STUDIES IN NEW TESTAMENT ETHICS

STUDIES IN
NEW TESTAMENT ETHICS

WILLIAM LILLIE

THE WESTMINSTER PRESS
PHILADELPHIA

Published in Great Britain by
Oliver and Boyd Ltd. Edinburgh and London 1961

First American Edition   1963
Library of Congress Catalog Card No. 63-7504

PRINTED IN GREAT BRITAIN BY OLIVER AND BOYD LTD., EDINBURGH

TO
FLORENCE JEAN

Acknowledgments

THIS book is the outcome of an invitation to give fifteen lectures on Christian Ethics to the students of the Presbyterian College, Belfast, and I have to thank very warmly the Faculty of the College, and particularly its Secretary, the Very Rev. Professor R. J. Wilson, for this invitation and for the great kindness shown to me during a very happy three weeks in the fellowship of the Presbyterian College in the early summer of 1960. I have also to thank those who have read my typescript and made many useful suggestions: my former colleague the Rev. Robert Davidson, now of the University of St Andrews, my wife, and Miss Anne Orde of Messrs Oliver and Boyd, who has given much more help and interest than an author could have expected from his publishers.

Unless otherwise indicated, Scripture quotations are taken from the Revised Standard Version of the Bible, copyright 1946 and 1952 by the Division of Christian Education, National Council of the Churches of Christ in the U.S.A., and used by permission. Chapter XV has already appeared in the *Scottish Journal of Theology* and is now reproduced with the Editors' permission. Grateful acknowledgment is made to all those, of whose writings I have made use, particularly the Rev. C. A. Pierce in Chapter V and the Rev. Professor Alan Richardson in Chapter X. Permission to quote has been kindly given in the case of longer quotations by the S.C.M. Press Ltd., for extracts from C. A. Pierce's *Conscience in the New Testament* in Chapter V, by Harper and Brothers, New York, for the quotation from A. N. Wilder's *Eschatology and Ethics in the New Testament* on page 146, and by Methuen and Co. Ltd., for the quotation from Dorothy L. Sayers' *The Six Other Deadly Sins* on page 99.

Contents

I	The Old Testament Heritage	I
II	Natural Law and the New Testament	12
III	The Example of Christ	24
IV	Grace and Goodness	34
V	Conscience in the New Testament	45
VI	Goodness and Knowledge	57
VII	The New Testament Attitude to Law and Justice	69
VIII	The New Testament Attitude to the State	82
IX	The New Testament Attitude to Wealth	93
X	The New Testament Attitude to Work	105
XI	The New Testament Attitude to Marriage and Divorce	118
XII	The New Testament Attitude to Children	129
XIII	Eschatology and Ethics in the New Testament	140
XIV	The Christian Conception of Self-denial	151
XV	The Christian Conception of Love	163
	List of Abbreviated Titles used in Notes	182
	Index of Scripture Passages	183

Chapter I

The Old Testament Heritage

ON the walls of many churches there are inscribed the Ten Commandments—a permanent witness to the fact that our Christian moral tradition owes much to the religion of the Old Testament. Many people today consider it to be "more Christian" to substitute for the Ten Commandments the two commandments of love which Jesus put first, but these too are derived from ancient Hebrew codes, the commandment to love God from the Deuteronomic Code (Dt. vi.5), and the commandment to love our neighbour from the Holiness Code of Leviticus (Lev. xix.18). Nor should it be forgotten that these codes are the later developments of a legal tradition that can in part be traced back far beyond the Biblical revelation to earlier Near Eastern civilisations. The moral reformer, and even more the founder of a new religion, must be tempted to try to shatter the moral universe of his time to bits so as to remould it nearer to his heart's desire, but, if he be wise, he resists this temptation. Our Lord might well have discarded the whole moral tradition of the Jews in view of what the Pharisees had made of it, but He explicitly stated that He had not come to abolish the law and the prophets but to fulfil them. "For truly, I say to you, till heaven and earth pass away, not an iota, not a dot, will pass from the law until all is accomplished" (Mt. v.18). This is the vivid hyperbole of an Eastern teacher, but it does drive home the truth that the ethics of the New Testament are firmly grounded in the revelation given in the Old Testament.

§ 2

The ethic of the Old Testament differs from most of the systems with which students of ethics are familiar, in basing human morality on Divine morality. This is strikingly expressed in the Holiness Code, both in the general injunction, "You shall be holy; for I the Lord your God am holy" (Lev. XIX.2), and in the adding to each particular commandment of the sanction, "I am the Lord your God." The root significance of *qadosh*, the Hebrew word translated "holy," is that which is separate or cut off from all profane use and content. Since Rudolf Otto wrote his *Idea of the Holy* scholars have tended to stress the non-moral implications of this word, the "wholly other," the "tremendous and fascinating mystery," and the "numinous," as Otto calls it. These implications are there, and there are places in Scripture where the meaning of *qadosh* seems limited to what is *tabu* or magically dangerous, as in the Ark stories in Samuel (I Sam. v; II Sam. VI.6-9). Yet this is not the paramount emphasis of the Old Testament. Even in two passages used by Otto to illustrate the numinous, Isaiah's vision in the Temple and Job's vision of the works of God in nature, it is to the moral nature of God that these men react. Isaiah's response is; "Woe is me! For I am lost; for I am a man of unclean lips, and I dwell in the midst of a people of unclean lips; for my eyes have seen the King, the Lord of hosts!" (Is. VI.5). Job's reaction is similar; "I had heard of thee by the hearing of the ear, but now my eye sees thee; therefore I despise myself, and repent in dust and ashes" (Job XLII.5, 6). When St Peter in the New Testament faces the numinous event of the miraculous draught of fishes, he has a similar response; "Depart from me, for I am a sinful man, O Lord" (Lk. v.8). What is evident in these examples is how closely the ethical is linked to the numinous; the response to the revelation of God's mysterious holiness is a deep sense of one's own sinfulness. It is never possible to think of God's holiness in purely ethical terms; His very goodness is a *mysterium tremendum*.

We may find some implications of this holiness of God relevant to our present conditions.

1. As is evident from our three examples, men who apprehend the holiness of God are filled with a sense of their own sinfulness, and indeed, as in Isaiah's case, the sinfulness of their community. This sense of sin is very repugnant to natural man, and the modern humanist will have none of it.

Yet this sense of sin is likely to be the most practical contribution that Christian morality has today to make to both industrial and international peace. When the Christian moralist intervenes in such matters, he is faced with technicalities he cannot understand, and claims and counter-claims of justice which only a specialist can evaluate. What the Christian does know for certain is that there is a measure of wrong—a coming short of the purpose of God—on both sides, and the realisation of this is the first necessary step towards reconciliation.

2. A second outcome of the holiness of God is the challenge to men to imitate it. This appears to be the implication of the verse we have quoted from the Holiness Code: "You shall be holy; for I the Lord your God am holy." Such an imitation of God is directly commanded in the Sermon on the Mount; "You, therefore, must be perfect, as your heavenly Father is perfect" (Mt. v.48), whether the word translated "perfect" be taken to mean "merciful," as in Luke, or "all-embracing," as some scholars believe the original Aramaic to have meant. The fact that we copy a transcendent God gives an other-worldly atmosphere to Christian morality. This is altogether opposed to the unfortunate tendency today for Christians, and even Christian ministers, to find some virtue in conforming to the world's standards, a process that might be aptly described as "keeping down with the Joneses." Many imagine that by so doing they will enjoy a more real fellowship with their worldly neighbours, and even influence them in the ways of Christ. The danger is that the "numinous" other-worldly aspect of Christian goodness is forgotten, and its beauty and mystery are lost.

3. More generally, the mighty acts of God demand an appropriate response on our part. The supreme example of this—and it is the very core of the Old Testament—is God's deliverance of Israel from Egypt seen as a demand for obedience and loyalty. This deliverance was not only a general challenge; the particular quality of God's action determined particular responses. When the Deuteronomic Code, for example, laid down the conditions on which a slave was to be set free, it said; "You shall remember that you were a slave in the land of Egypt, and the Lord your God redeemed you; therefore I command you today" (Dt. xv.15). Brunner finds here

the special characteristic of Christian ethics; it is "the science of human conduct as it is determined by Divine conduct."[1]

§ 3

God's holiness, as determinative of man's conduct, is spoken of in the Old Testament chiefly in terms of justice, mercy, and truth.[2] A common misrepresentation, heard in the pulpit as well as the marketplace, is that, while the New Testament presents a God of forgiveness and compassion, the Old Testament presents a God of vengeance and wrath. It may be that some Old Testament writers, like some twentieth-century preachers in time of war, confused their own national causes with the righteous purposes of God, so that vengeance obliterated mercy; but by and large, even in the Old Testament, there is no inconsistency between God's justice and God's mercy.

It is true that the moralist studying justice in the Old Testament may receive some surprises. The "judges" of the book called by that name, are notoriously warriors delivering their tribes from hostile attacks rather than magistrates deciding cases, although some of them do administer justice rather as a side-line. *Shophet*, the Hebrew word for such a warrior "judge," is of the same root as *mishpat*, the word used for a legal decision taken as a precedent. Again *tsedaqah*, the Hebrew word translated "righteousness," although it was probably derived from a root meaning "straight," often seems to imply a bias in favour of the widow, the orphan, and the alien—the common victims of oppression—and the justice of a judge includes his consideration for such people as well as his adherence to abstract principles of equity. The righteous God, and the righteous man, is, like the *shophet*, the vindicator of, and the winner of victories for, his people. In the song of Deborah, the righteousnesses of Yahweh are simply military triumphs (Jg. v.11), and in a later prophet, a "righteous" man appears to mean a victor, with no moral significance at all (Is. XLIX.24).

Behind the various meanings of righteousness and judgment is a picture of a king administering justice very different from

[1] E. Brunner, *The Divine Imperative*, London 1937, p. 86. Translation of *Das Gebot und die Ordnungen*, 2nd edn. Tübingen 1933.
[2] N. H. Snaith, *The Distinctive Ideas of the Old Testament*, London 1944, Chs. 3-5.

our modern ideas. Today we limit the work of a judge to the giving of correct legal decisions, and we think that a personal interest in the offender before him is likely to bias his judgment. We may admit that the ultimate function of the ruler or magistrate is to maintain the stability of his people. He may do this, as a modern judge does, by punishing offenders, but, in the conditions of ancient Israel, he did it even more often by delivering his people from their enemies. When the case of an individual came before him, the righteous judge showed a personal interest and concern for this individual; some of the stories of the Arabian Nights show how much this is expected of a good Eastern ruler. In such a situation, the declaring of a man innocent or "righteous" is no mere formal acquittal; it expresses a personal approval of the man, that may secure for him not merely escape from punishment, but protection from his enemies and liberation for a new way of life. So God's righteousness "not only liberates; it is righteousness in action which, after having humbled man under its royal authority, lifts him up and assists him to live better."[3] We shall see later[4] that the similar view of justice in the New Testament is directly relevant to our modern treatment of offenders; the liberation of the individual has a place here as well as the stability of the community.

The mercy of God is denoted in the Old Testament by a very frequently used but almost untranslateable Hebrew word, *hesed*. Scholars are agreed that this is the virtue which gives stability to a covenant relationship, not by way of legal sanction, but by way of personal love. So the older translators make it "lovingkindness" or "mercy," while modern translators make it "steadfast love" (R.S.V.), "leal love" (G. A. Smith), or "covenant love" (N. H. Snaith). There was bound to develop a difference in emphasis in the word when applied to God, whose *hesed* is shown in mercy and grace, and when applied to man, whose *hesed* is shown in dutiful obedience. Yet *hesed* is fundamentally the same quality whether in God or in man; otherwise two different words would have been used. Just as our

---

[3] P. Bonnard, "Righteous," in *Vocabulary of the Bible*, ed. J. J. von Allmen, London 1958, p. 373. Translation of *Vocabulaire biblique*, 2nd edn. Neuchâtel and Paris 1956. Cf. Ps. CXLIII.

[4] Chapter VII.

human justice must resemble Divine justice in a personal concern for the individual's deliverance, so our human mercy must resemble the Divine mercy. In particular, it must show the qualities of steadfastness and dependability, removing from it the arbitrariness and caprice which so often characterise mere human acts of kindness. There is in the Old Testament notion of *hesed* an anticipation of our Lord's teaching on forgiveness; "For if you forgive men their trespasses, your heavenly Father also will forgive you; but if you do not forgive men their trespasses, neither will your Father forgive your trespasses" (Mt. VI.14, 15). There must be something—*hesed* or forgiveness—shared by God and man to make the covenant relationship effective.

In mentioning stability, we have indicated a third aspect of God's holiness, which characterises His justice and His mercy. Linked with *hesed*, and sometimes not far from it in meaning, are the qualities of truth (*'emeth*) and faithfulness (*'emunah*). One of these two is found along with *hesed* in twenty-three Old Testament passages,[5] and this goes to confirm that steadfastness is one element in *hesed*. The common root of *'emeth* and *'emunah*, is used in connexion with a mother's care. "The vivid picture of the constancy and steadfastness of a parent to her child lurks behind the Old Testament conception of faithfulness."[6] When St Paul gives in Romans his characteristic presentation of the Gospel message, he uses as His text Hab. II.4; "The righteous shall live by his *'emunah*." We need not be greatly concerned as to whether this word denotes faithfulness as an attribute of God or faith as an attitude of human trust, for it is fundamental to Biblical ethics that human faith is altogether dependent on God's faithfulness. We trust Him, because He is wholly trustworthy. He is the faithful and the true.

Protestant theologians today tend to relegate Christian ethics to a very subordinate place in a theology which has as its core "justification by faith alone" as taught by St Paul and the Reformers. What they tend to ignore is the fact that there is an ethical element right at the heart of this doctrine. It all rests on the faithfulness or steadfastness of God exhibited

---

[5] Snaith, *Distinctive Ideas of the Old Testament*, p. 100.
[6] Ruth IV.16; Is. LX.4. T. F. Torrance in *Expository Times*, LXVIII (1957), p. 111.

both in His justice and in His mercy; without them there would be no Gospel of salvation. These, however transcendent they may be in God, are qualities common to God and man. When a man responds to the challenge of these qualities in God's action, his response, while including other elements, has certainly as one part the appropriating to himself of the moral qualities of God. This gift is given sometimes through conscious imitation, sometimes through secret influence. God's justice demands man's justice; God's forgiveness demands man's forgiveness; and God's faithfulness in the Old Testament does not lose all ethical content when it finds a response in New Testament faith. This is no mere academic speculation about the frontiers between morality and religion or between theology and ethics. When in our straightforward evangel we call men to *believe* in the Lord Jesus Christ, we are calling them to share responsively in the steadfastness and reliability which God Himself has shown in the whole Biblical revelation. Faith is more than an act of existential decision, just as it is more than the mere intellectual assent of belief; it is a whole-hearted loyalty to God, bestowed by Him and worked out in daily living. There is no more necessary application of New Testament ethics today than the recovery in our preaching and in our practice of the unity of faith and faithfulness.

§ 4

The Old Testament is often charged with a narrow nationalism in its moral outlook. The Hebrews certainly regarded themselves as a holy people apart from other nations, but even from the time of Abraham an obligation to other nations was recognised; this is certainly one implication of the obscure saying that all the families of the earth would find a blessing in Abraham's seed (Gen. xii.3, etc.). Christianity rightly sees itself as a religion with no national limitations, and believes that the obligations, which in the Old Testament and other ancient codes are limited to one's own fellow countrymen, are obligations to all human beings of every race.

This emphasis on ethical universalism must not blind us to the fact that the "people of God" is an Old Testament notion which Christianity has not abandoned. The Church,

B

which is of course not limited to any national group, is the true Israel, the people whom God has chosen for Himself in the New Age. God's election of a chosen people, which many Churches accept in their credal statements as a theological doctrine, is often neglected in Christian ethics. Its ethical importance is suggested in the Johannine writings, where love of the brethren or the mutual love of disciples to one another is given a larger place than the love to all men which is taught elsewhere in the New Testament. This has often been regarded as a concession by John to the smallness of men's hearts. Yet the fact of the Church, whether we call it the body of Christ or the people of God, must mean that its members have obligations of love, loyalty and service to one another, different from those which they undoubtedly have to all men. There need be nothing self-centred about such obligations within the fellowship; indeed it is just because the Church has a mission of unselfish service to the world that the relations of its members to one another are so important. "By this all men will know that you are my disciples, if you have love for one another" (Jn. XIII.35).

The sense of corporate unity, which the Church has inherited as the successor of Israel, did not prevent in the Old Testament story a strong sense of individual rights, and it is to Hebrew practice more than to Greek theory that modern democracy owes its emphasis on the freedom and equality of individual men and women—an emphasis which the Church has forgotten at certain periods of her history. Psalmists and prophets recognise that, along with the obligations of individuals, the people of Israel had as a corporate personality certain responsibilites. The Church has similar responsibilities, one of which is to make up her mind and to make clear pronouncements on the moral issues involved in political and social questions. It is a sad fact that the Church speaks today with a divided voice on many moral issues; for such issues are certainly involved in political decisions on nuclear armaments or in legislation on gambling. We are apt to excuse this division of opinion within the Church as an unavoidable consequence of the liberty of opinion which, at least since the eighteenth century, has been regarded in Protestant countries as part of our Christian heritage. Yet it does suggest that the Church as a body is not listening to the Word of God in humble obedience. It was when the Hebrew people failed to listen to that Word spoken by the prophets that they lost their ability to make the clear witness to the world that they should have done.

§ 5

The idea of a covenant is fundamental in Old Testament ethics. As we have seen, the chosen people are the people of the covenant and *hesed* is "covenant love," the proper mutual feeling of parties to one another within a covenant. God's justice is shown both in defending and vindicating His own people within the covenant, and in His faithful dealings with them and discipline of them. The word "covenant" is sometimes used in the Old Testament for a merely human agreement or a legal contract between two parties (Gen. XXXI.44; 1 Sam. XVIII.3). Even in these very human covenants, the personal element is generally more conspicuous than it is in a modern contract, and God enters into the covenant as the authority providing sanctions for its observance (Gen. XXXI.50, 53; 1 Sam. XX.8, 13-16). The most important covenants of the Old Testament are, however, covenants made by God, above all that which He made with the Hebrews at Mount Sinai (Ex. XXIV.1-8), a covenant which was frequently remembered and renewed throughout Old Testament history (Josh. XXIV.25; II Kings XXIII.3; Neh. IX.38), and which serves as a type of the new covenant predicted by Jeremiah (Jer. XXXI.31) and fulfilled in the New Testament (1 Cor. XI.25). If ordinary covenants between men in Old Testament times were more personal than their modern counterparts, still less was the Sinai Covenant, which gives the Old Testament its name, a merely legal compact. It was sealed by a religious rite, the blood of the covenant being sprinkled on God's altar and on the human party (Ex. XXIV.6, 8). It was a covenant initiated by Yahweh as an act of His grace. "He did not impose it, but out of grace he offered it. The advantages were great, because the acceptance meant the bestowal of blessing from Yahweh, a blessing which included the gift of an 'inheritance,' security from enemies, law and order. . . . Israel on her part freely accepted the covenant, but in doing so solemnly placed herself under obligation to obey the Ruler and the law which he gave as the constitution of the society."[7]

It has been a favourite theory of moral philosophers that morality depends on a social contract of one kind or another. Whatever can be said for or against this view in the case of ordinary secular morals and "natural law" theories, it is certain that Christian morality, like the morality of the Old Testament before it, is morality within a covenant, but a covenant of a very special kind that would probably have shocked Hobbes, Rousseau, and their company. It is a covenant initiated by God, so that the justice and mercy which it demands in human relationships are demanded and guaranteed by the justice and mercy of God Himself. It is not a covenant which is imposed on men against their will. G. E. Wright says of the Old Covenant and Law; "They were God's gift of life,"[8] and this is still more true of the New Covenant. Whatever moral obligations the New Testament demands—and it does make such demands—God's service remains, in the words of a beautiful collect, "perfect freedom." The obligations entailed by such a covenant are obligations both for the community as a whole and for the individuals composing it. Achan's disobedience brought the whole Hebrew community near to disaster (Josh. vii), and the disloyalty of an individual today can still make a breach in the covenant relationship of God and His Church. Theologians today give the first place to God's part in the Covenant, and this is right, so long as they remember that one thing that God does is to invite men to accept the grace which will enable them to fulfil the moral demands that He makes in the Covenant. For God still asks for His own justice and mercy, His own faithfulness and love to be found in those who are the people of His Covenant.

[7] G. E. Wright, *The Old Testament against its Environment*, Studies in Biblical Theology VOL. II, London 1950, p. 58.
[8] G. E. Wright, *op cit.*, p. 58.

Literature

N. H. SNAITH, *The Distinctive Ideas of the Old Testament*, London 1944.

R. OTTO, *The Idea of the Holy*, London 1928. Translation of *Das Heilige*.

R. DAVIDSON, "Some aspects of the Old Testament contribution to the pattern of Christian ethics," in *Scottish Journal of Theology*, XII (1959), pp. 373-87.

G. E. WRIGHT, *The Old Testament against its Environment*, Studies in Biblical Theology VOL. II, London 1950.

G. E. MENDENHALL, *Law and Covenant in Israel and the Ancient Near East*, Pittsburg 1955.

Chapter II

Natural Law and the New Testament

NATURAL LAW may be defined as a universal standard of conduct, morally binding on all men and directly discernible by them.[1] C. S. Lewis describes it as "the human idea of Decent Behaviour . . . obvious to everyone."[2] The content of this law is much more difficult to determine. "To render to each man his due"—*suum cuique tribuere*—is, according to Brunner and others, the "real content" of the Law of Nature.[3] Others, like the Scholastic philosophers, add a negative content, "to hurt no-one"—*neminem laedere*.[4] These two Latin tags represent philosophers' attempts to find universal principles in the rather vague ideas of what is right, common to all normal people. Lord Stair, the Scottish jurist, included in the Law of Nature "the common practical principles that God is to be obeyed, parents honoured, ourselves defended, violence repulsed, children to be loved, educated and provided for."[5] Ellul points out that in all societies there are rules, not technically identical, but relating to the same institutions and the same juridic reality, with regard to such things as marriage, parental authority, slavery, property, murder, theft, contracts, and pledges.[6] The sphere of Natural Law is evidently very wide.

Of the fact that there are such widespread ideas of what is just or right there can be no doubt. In the New Testament even the Gentiles know wrong-doing when they see it (1 Pet. II.12), and St Paul gives examples of the natural right of a

---

[1] A. R. Vidler and W. A. Whitehouse, *Natural Law*, London 1946, p. 13.

[2] C. S. Lewis, *Broadcast Talks*, London 1942, p. 10.

[3] Brunner, *Divine Imperative*, p. 628.

[4] J. Ellul, *The Theological Foundation of Law*, henceforth cited as *Theological Foundation*, London 1961, p. 23. Translation of *Le Fondement théologique du droit*, Neuchâtel 1946.

[5] Quoted by T. M. Taylor, *The Discipline of Virtue*, London 1954, p. 27.

[6] Ellul, *Theological Foundation*, p. 28 f.

man to get a just return for his labours (1 Cor. IX.7). There are, however, very different theories of Natural Law, explaining these universally shared notions of what is right. Those who deny that there is any such thing as Natural Law regard these notions as having arisen in different civilisations and at different periods because of similar external circumstances or even by sheer coincidence. The Stoic theory, which has dominated philosophical and legal studies of the subject, finds the source of Natural Law in the universal reason that is common to all men. The definition, with which this chapter began, in its original form made Natural Law "discernible *by the light of reason*;" I removed the word "reason" to avoid an uncritical acceptance of the Stoic theory. The Christian theory of Natural Law, according to Brunner, finds it to be "simply and solely the order of creation. . . . The natural man was well aware of these orders of creation though without knowing the Creator" [7] The early Christians, including the writers of the New Testament, were probably influenced by the eclectic Stoicism which was then part of the common thought of the Hellenistic world, and they were certainly influenced by the Old Testament doctrine of Creation. It is extremely unlikely that they had a clear conception or theory of Natural Law. They probably talked about it in the unscholarly way that people today talk about "evolution." What they knew and what we still know, is that there are some things everybody knows to be wrong and others everybody knows to be right. What St Paul saw was the primacy of the principle (also put first by Lord Stair) that "God is to be obeyed." The notions of the pagan world about what is natural had gone all wrong because of their failure to know and obey God (Rom. 1.18-32).

§ 2

The *locus classicus* for the teaching of Natural Law in the New Testament is Rom. II.14-16. It begins; "When Gentiles who have not the law do by nature what the law requires, they are a law to themselves, even though they do not have the law." Our modern way of putting this would be to say that it is a fact of experience that people who do not know the

[7] E. Brunner, *Justice and the Social Order*, Eng. trans., London 1946, p. 84.

Ten Commandments do commonly practise such things as a rudimentary honesty and submission to parents. St Paul suggests that they do this by instinct ("nature"), and that this instinct does for the pagan in some limited measure what the law of Moses does for the Jew, so that "they are a law to themselves, even though they do not have the law." St Paul goes on to say; "They show that what the law requires is written on their hearts, while their conscience also bears witness and their conflicting thoughts accuse or perhaps excuse them on that day when, according to my gospel, God judges the secrets of men by Christ Jesus." The pagan may act after a debate in his mind, in which both his conscience and his thoughts take part, providing arguments for and against the action.[8] His conscience is here obviously not a direct insight into the dictates of Natural Law, and his thoughts, so far from being the calm reason of the Stoics, are in conflict with one another. Yet the fact that the pagan sometimes does the right thing shows that the instinct—the "law written on the heart"—is there and sometimes has its way. This will be made clear on the day "when God judges the secrets of men by Christ Jesus." This last judgment is for St Paul far more definite than those of natural instinct, conscience, or reason.

St Paul here introduces the notion of Natural Law for the special purpose of showing that Jews and Gentiles are equally sinners before God. For this argument, Gentiles must be assumed to have something analogous to the law of Moses, and the idea of a "law written on the heart" is ready to hand. Yet St Paul is not too happy with this notion. The good pagan is influenced in his choice of good by other factors, such as the pains of conscience and his own mental deliberations, as well as by the natural instinct, which is only a law in a figurative sense. (St Paul must have known also that pagans, good and bad alike, were influenced by the laws of the society in which they lived and the moral atmosphere of that society generally, but he ignores this as irrelevant to his argument here.) St Paul is well aware that none of these can guarantee the ultimate validity of a moral judgment; that is reserved for the judgment seat of Christ. He accepts, as all must, Natural Law as a fact; men do have some ideas in common about what

[8] Ellul, *Theological Foundation*, p. 89.

is right. He has little to offer in the way of an explanatory
theory.

What the New Testament suggests as a theory of Natural
Law is that there are certain institutions or orders of community
demanding those relationships which are embodied in Natural
Law. Marriage depends on the fact that "from the beginning
of creation God made them male and female" (Mk. x.6);
"every family in heaven and on earth is named" from the
Heavenly Father (Eph. iii.15); and the "governing authorities"
like the state, have been "instituted by God" (Rom. xiii.1).
Ellul says that these are creations of God just as much as light
or trees, quite independent of human volition.[9] Modern
thinkers differ from one another about how directly Natural
Law is given in these institutions, and the New Testament
simply takes it for granted that they imply such things as
monogamous marriage and submission to government. The
Bible has a myth of a perfect natural order in the garden of
Eden before the Fall, not unlike the Stoic myth of a primeval
Golden Age found in Seneca,[10] but the New Testament writers
look forward to a heavenly city rather than backward to a
garden of Eden. Yet, as we have seen, it was to the Genesis
myth that our Lord appealed in His repudiation of divorce.
Whether or not we believe that He accepted the historicity of
the myth, He certainly accepted God's created order as in
some way determinative of what is right. God made men and
women in such fashion that a life-long union is the only natural
marriage relationship.

St Paul similarly appealed to nature in his discussion on
the vices of the heathen in Rom. 1. One example of their
degradation is that "their women exchanged natural relations
for unnatural, and the men likewise gave up natural relations
with women and were consumed with passion for one another"
(Rom. 1.26, 27). The philosopher Kant made a distinction
between *crimina secundum naturam* and *crimina contra naturam*, the
latter being not only contrary to reason as developed in our
moral codes, but also "contrary to natural instinct and to
animal nature." About these Kant echoes St Paul's words;
"Human beings feel, therefore, ashamed to mention those

[9] Ellul, *Theological Foundation*, p. 71 f.
[10] Seneca, *Epistle* xc.

things of which it is shameful for humanity to be capable."[11]
Our Lord's teaching on divorce and St Paul's teaching in
Rom. 1 both support Kant here and show that New Testament
morality has some basis in the natural order of things.

Today the sophisticated can present very specious arguments to justify many vices. Homosexuality, they say, is as
natural as heterosexuality. We need not doubt that Christ
feels for the man of perverted instincts as great a compassion as
He did for the woman caught in the act of adultery, and it is
not for us to judge how far the pervert is sick or insane; that
is the business of the psychiatrist. What we as Christians must
maintain is that the use of sex for other purposes than those
for which the plain man sees it was obviously intended is
wrong, and wrong because it is unnatural. From the beginning
it was not so! Our Lord with His perfect insight seems to have
seen divorce as something similarly unnatural, although few
men are clear-sighted enough to share His reaction here. It
would be wrong to ignore the complexities and obscurities of
many moral situations, but it does appear from the New Testament that there are certain practices which the simple, honest
man sees to be "against nature" and so wrong.

§ 3

Our Lord's admission that Moses had to modify the "Natural
Law" regarding marriage because of the hardness of men's
hearts illustrates what has been called the relative law or the
secondary law of nature, which is the Law of Nature as applicable to man, no longer enjoying the Golden Age, but a fallen
creature in a fallen world. The relative law "is not a law at
all," says Brunner, "it simply expresses the necessity . . . of
adapting the absolute Law of Nature to the sinful reality."[12]
The institution of private property, (which Seneca believed to
be absent in his Golden Age), the "just war," and the right
to divorce one's partner in marriage are examples of the
changes that the Fall has brought about in men's ideas of
what is naturally right. Yet, throughout the New Testament,
there are what we might interpret as aspirations to the primeval

---

[11] I. Kant, *Lectures on Ethics*, Eng. trans., London 1930, p. 169; cf. Eph. v.12
[12] Brunner, *Divine Imperative*, p. 630.

perfections of the absolute Law of Nature, although the early Christians did not think of them as such. We find these aspirations in the attempted community of goods in the early Jerusalem Church, in those sayings of our Lord commonly quoted by pacifists,[13] and most conspicuously in our Lord's teaching on divorce. This is important for our Christian ethics today. It is obvious that we have to live our lives in the relativities of our present moral atmosphere and most Christians feel that they have to accept such things as the capitalist system, conscription for military service in wartime, and taxation for purposes of which we do not approve. Similarly the apostles, and Christians right up to the nineteenth century, appear to have accepted slavery as a necessary institution in a fallen world, although they might have admitted that it was contrary both to the original Law of Nature and to the mind of Christ. It is right and proper that there should be Christians in this as in every age with aspirations to the original order of nature, even if men label them eccentrics or heretics. It will be an ill day for the Church and for the world when there are no pacifists, no idealists attempting communistic experiments, and no High Churchmen whole-heartedly repudiating divorce in any form.

In Stoic thought, the principles of Natural Law were discernible by human reason, and this tradition is still deeply imbedded in the Roman Catholic doctrine of Natural Law. Our Lord's statement that spiritual truths may be hidden from the wise and prudent but revealed to babes (Mt. xi.25) reminds us of the limitations of human reason. Yet it is easy to go too far and to regard all the reasonings of fallen men as futile and self-deceiving. The New Testament itself constantly challenges its readers to use their reasoning powers, for example in our Lord's parables and in St Paul's doctrinal arguments. There is much in the Gospel, particularly in the strange parable of the Unjust Steward, to suggest that God means men to use their intelligence in ordering their conduct. Yet human reason can go far astray under the influence of sin; as St Paul put it, men can "hold down the truth in unrighteousness" (Rom. i.18, R.V.). It is through a glass darkly that our human reason at its best discerns the Law of Nature.

[13] E.g. Mt. v.39, xxvi.52; Jn. xviii.36.

It is notorious that men often confuse what is conventional or "what is always done" with what is natural, and unfortunately there seems to be a glaring example of this confusion in the New Testament itself. St Paul asks; "Does not nature itself teach you that for a man to wear long hair is degrading to him, but if a woman has long hair, it is her pride?" (1 Cor. xi.14-15). St Paul appears to have forgotten the Nazirites and the other virile individualists who have on principle refused to use a razor. St Paul does seem to be conscious of some weakness in his argument here, for he refuses to hear any objection to it. "If any one is disposed to be contentious, we recognize no other practice, nor do the churches of God" (vs. 16). Modern man still confuses what is always done with what is right. Men will always gamble on something, they say, therefore gambling cannot be wrong, or even, like St Paul, women must not come to church without hats, for that has always been the practice of the churches of God. The command to follow nature might more logically lead to the practice of nudism than to St Paul's injunction to employ a barber.

In view of these qualifications, it appears that the writers of the New Testament accept the fact of Natural Law, and even use Natural Law arguments incidentally to enforce particular points, but that their primary ethical interests are elsewhere. What had been fundamental in Jewish ethics was the law of Moses directly given by God, and what would take its place, while it would be a law written on men's hearts in the sense of preferring the spirit to the letter (Jer. xxxi.33), was as definitely God's command as had been the law of Moses. Jesus Himself made this perfectly clear, and men marvelled at His authority. Indeed, it is only because Natural Law also is God-given, although in men's understanding less directly, that it has any place in the New Testament at all.

§ 4

We use today the phrase "natural law" or "law of nature" ambiguously. Moralists still use it for the universal standard of conduct binding on all men, but others use it more commonly for a scientific generalisation, "a general proposition . . . that certain relations always hold in certain cases."[14]   This ambiguity may have some part in the popular, but fallacious, belief that what is natural is always right.   Neither New Testament teaching nor the Christian doctrine of Natural Law gives any grounds for this view.   "At all times what has been meant by the Law of Nature is a *moral* principle of justice which subjects and regulates the natural instinct of man, whether it be the instinct of power, of gain, of sex.   It has never acknowledged that instinct as a principle of action or of judgment."[15] Scripture suggests a reason for this; the natural instinct of man has been corrupted by the Fall, or, as St Paul has it, man is the slave of sin, "sold under sin."

In the Bible what we call law, whether moral or scientific, is regarded primarily as God's command.   It was by God's fiat that the natural order began; "And God said, 'Let there be light'; and there was light" (Gen. 1.3).   Equally, every moral law is God's command; in the Holiness Code of Leviticus, each moral precept finds its authority in the statement; "I am the Lord."   Christian thinkers commonly find the same permanence and immutability in moral and scientific law. "The law of righteousness is as inexorable as the law of gravitation,"[16] or, as Brunner puts it, "The Eternal Divine plan . . . because it is unchangeable, is called *lex*."[17]   We need to be reminded that God's commands are not arbitrary and capricious, as many people today imagine them to be.   On the other hand one of the dangers of both natural science and ethics is that they depersonalise the relationships of the universe. The New Testament never does this.   It is God who "makes his sun rise on the evil and on the good, and sends rain on the just and on the unjust" (Mt. v.45).   Equally it is God who gives the Ten Commandments, and the new commandment of love. There is the further danger in this analogy that we consider the laws of morality to be as unchangeable as we (perhaps wrongly) suppose the laws of nature to be, and so leave no room for the indeterminate possibilities of new creative achievements in the moral life.   This open range of new

[14] A. D. Ritchie, *Scientific Method*, London 1923, p. 35.
[15] Brunner, *Justice and the Social Order*, p. 81.
[16] N. Micklem, *Law and the Laws*, Edinburgh 1952, p. 32.
[17] Brunner, *Divine Imperative*, p. 628.

possibilities was what our Lord envisaged in the Sermon on the Mount when He passed from what was said to the men of old to what "I say to you."

In spite of our denial that what is natural is necessarily right, it is possible to see something of a common pattern in nature and in morality. It was this which enabled our Lord to use the common things of nature as vehicles of spiritual truths in His parables, and which makes possible sacramental views of the universe. A striking example is our Lord's use of a grain of wheat, falling into the ground and dying and so bearing much fruit. This, while typifying His own death on the Cross, immediately leads to the moral teaching; "He who loves his life loses it, and he who hates his life in this world will keep it for eternal life" (Jn. xii.24-5). Self-denial and love[18] are as truly developments of what is given in nature, as the unrestrained sexuality and the egotistic aggressiveness that are commonly defended as natural today.

§ 5

C. H. Dodd holds "that the ethical teaching given by the early church was pretty closely related to the general movement in Graeco-Roman society towards the improvement of public morals as it was undertaken in the first century by various agencies. Christian teachers took for granted the existing structure of society, with its known moral problems and dangers. Up to a point, they were able to adopt a good deal of the basic criticism and counsel which serious moralists of other schools were urging on their contemporaries".[19] The ethical teaching of the early Christians came primarily from the Old Testament tradition which shared, too, the insights of Natural Law, and at the same time could criticise and refine these insights in the light of the revealed Torah. Of course the Christians had new insights and saw new possibilities, but it was not their business to devise an entirely new morality, altogether different from that of the Jews or that of the Stoics. The Natural Law, however much it has been corrupted in the

---

[18] M. D'Arcy in *Mind and Heart of Love*, London 1945, regards *agape* as the flowering of the feminine principle in human nature.

[19] C. H. Dodd, *Gospel and Law*, Cambridge, 1951, pp. 23f.

hearts of fallen men, still means that there is a common element in all human codes of morality, and, as Dodd says, it is part of the Church's mission "to bear witness to this aboriginal law of man's creation."[20]

This is worth emphasising today. Not only the materialism and hedonism that vaguely permeate popular thinking but certain explicitly held doctrines are contrary both to Christian teaching and to Natural Law. The doctrine of racial *apartheid*, which is speciously based on biological facts, is not only a violation of the law of Christ; it is a contradiction of a truth realised both by Hebrew prophets and Stoic philosophers. It is because of what is common to Natural Law and Christian teaching that we Christians can put pressure on our legislators to embody certain Christian values in the laws of a society composed partly of unbelievers. Monogamy, for example, is not only the command of Christ; in spite of the polygamy practised by the patriarchs and by many old and stable societies in Asia and Africa, it was, as He suggested, part of the original order of creation. The acceptance of polygamy as "natural" is an instance of "adapting the absolute Law of Nature to the sinful reality." I have argued elsewhere[21] that gambling, particularly in the present-day form where gigantic sums are won from very small stakes, is a violation of the Natural Law of the just price, implicit in Biblical teaching but clearly enunciated by Aristotle. We Christians may have learned these things from our Bibles, but they are also implications of the Natural Law shared by all. Again, it is because of Natural Law that there can be so much co-operation between Christians and non-Christians in social service. Ellul thinks that this is a leading reason for the Christian emphasis on Natural Law, which can easily become a false over-emphasis.[22]

We must certainly not allow an emphasis on Natural Law to conceal certain essential elements in the Christian ethic. There is, as I suggested in the first chapter, a transcendent element in Biblical ethics, based on the holiness of God, which is repugnant to man's ordinary ways of thinking. There is an element of excess, as in the Father's attitude to the Prodigal

[20] C. H. Dodd, *Gospel and Law*, p. 82.
[21] W. Lillie, *The Law of Christ*, London 1956, Ch. VI.
[22] Ellul, *Theological Foundation*, p. 10.

Son or in our Lord's command to forgive seventy times seven, which contradicts the Greek doctrine of moderation which is much more acceptable to human reason. Nor can laws, even Natural Laws, take fully into account the personal concern for each individual which is fundamental to Christian morality. Law is not enough.

There are two kindred uses of Natural Law, for which there is little, if any, support in the New Testament. Both the Stoics and the men of the Enlightenment believed that they had in Natural Law a standard of justice, by which they could measure the justice of ordinary laws and institutions. Apart from the vagueness of the dictates of Natural Law, it may be argued, as by Ellul,[23] that, apart from revelation, man does not know real justice, but that what he calls justice is a pragmatic justice, by which he adapts himself to the conditions of life, including the institutions created by God. There is nothing in Romans to suggest that it is anything more.[24] The other use is as the ground of protest against tyranny. "Anyone," writes Brunner, "who is not prepared to come to terms with the legal monstrosity of the totalitarian state has no alternative but the right to resist based solely on the law of nature."[25] Negatively, this is correct; the final word is never with man-made law, however powerfully it be enforced. It is true that on one occasion, in the matter of divorce, our Lord did appeal from the positive laws of Judaism to the Natural Law that was from the beginning. Yet this is only a single instance, and it is hard to believe that St Paul would have in any circumstances considered Natural Law as an adequate basis of the right to resist the authorities instituted by God. Christ's own appeal would in such circumstances have been to the Will of my Father, who is in heaven. The justice to which the New Testament appeals is not manifested in a vague intuition, nor even in positive human law, but in what God Himself has done in visiting and redeeming His people. History provides evidence that great risings against totalitarian tyranny, such as the Reformation in Scotland was in great measure, have sprung not only from human ideas of natural justice,

---

[23] Ellul, *Theological Foundation*, pp. 85-93.
[24] Cf. Rom. ix.30, 31.
[25] Brunner, *Justice and the Social Order*, p. 88.

but also from a new understanding of the Will of God as revealed in His Word.

Literature

E. BRUNNER, *The Divine Imperative*, London 1937, pp. 627-33. Translation of *Das Gebot und die Ordnungen*, 2nd edn. Tübingen 1933.

E. BRUNNER, *Justice and the Social Order*, Eng. trans. London 1946, ch. XII.

J. ELLUL, *The Theological Foundation of Law*, London 1961. Translation of *Le Fondement théologique du droit*, Neuchâtel 1946.

J. DALBY, *The Catholic Conception of the Law of Nature*, London 1943.

A. R. VIDLER and W. A. WHITEHOUSE, *Natural Law*, London 1946.

A. P. D'ENTRÉVES, *Natural Law*, London 1951.

I. HENDERSON, *Can Two Walk Together?* London 1948.

Chapter III

The Example of Christ

A SPEAKER addressing a gathering of English Franciscans pointed out how very different St Francis was from our Lord. Many of his hearers were horrified at this statement, but in a certain sense the speaker was right. The proof of his assertion lies in the fact that those Christians who have been nearest in life and character to our Lord have been very different from one another. Even the glimpses that we have in the Gospels of the individual characteristics of apostles like Peter and Thomas and Andrew show them to be men with very different personalities.

Yet the teaching of the New Testament, and of Christian moralists ever since, is perfectly clear and straightforward; we are called to follow the example of Christ both in general principle and in particular ways of action. "Be ye imitators of me, as I am of Christ," wrote St Paul (1 Cor. xi.1), and the "imitator" in Greek as in English deliberately copies his pattern. Our Lord repeatedly told His disciples that any man who would join their company must take up his cross and follow Him (Mk. viii.34, etc.), and to follow means not only to take the same road, but to go about it in the same way. St Peter, writing to Christians who were being persecuted, commended to them the example of Jesus. "Christ also suffered for you, leaving you an example, that you should follow in his steps. He committed no sin; no guile was found on his lips. When he was reviled, he did not revile in return; when he suffered, he did not threaten; but he trusted to him who judges justly" (1 Pet. ii.21-3). Jesus gave His own meekness as an example to others. "Learn from me," He said, "for I am gentle and lowly in heart" (Mt. xi.29). His own love provided a pattern for the disciples' love; His new commandment was, "even as I have loved you, that you also love one another"[2] (Jn. xiii.34). St John saw as the goal of the Christian life that "we shall be like him," and "every one who thus hopes in him purifies himself as he is pure"[3] (1 Jn. iii.2, 3). Even about such a simple and commonplace action as washing His disciples' feet, Jesus said: "I have given you an example, that you also should do as I have done to you"[4] (Jn. xiii.15). The New Testament emphasis on the imitation of Christ has continued right down the centuries. It gave its name to one of the greatest Christian classics, and it is a frequent theme of modern hymns. There is a section in most hymn-books for hymns of our Lord's life and example, and their common prayer is, "Let Thy life our pattern be."

The outcome of this form of piety might appear to be that all Christians should follow one strictly uniform pattern of living. Our spirits revolt against such an idea, for life would be less interesting and less rich in content if all men were fashioned on the same mould like a regiment of toy soldiers. It is such a uniformity rather than its moral earnestness which has made Puritanism often so unattractive. We may believe that, just because we are individually different members of the body of Christ, we must be different from one another in order that each individual can best fulfil his own peculiar function within the body. George Macdonald was surely expressing a Christian truth when he wrote; "Every one of us is something that the other is not, and therefore knows something—it may be without knowing that he knows it—which no one else knows: and . . . it is every one's business, as one of the kingdom of light and inheritor in it all, to give his portion to the rest."[1]

§ 2

Christians are summoned to be imitators, not only of Jesus during His life on earth, but of God Himself. Jesus said; "You, therefore, must be perfect, as your heavenly Father is perfect" (Mt. v.48), or; "Be merciful, even as your Father is merciful" (Lk. vi.36), and St Paul exhorted his readers at Ephesus; "Be imitators of God, as beloved children" (Eph. v.1). If it is beyond our capacity to imitate Jesus of Nazareth

---

[1] C. S. Lewis, *George Macdonald, An Anthology*, London 1946, p. 98 f.

on earth, it is beyond our understanding even to think of
imitating God in heaven.   There is danger in it, too, for was
not it part of the temptation that first led man astray to desire
to be "like God, knowing good and evil"?   Yet it is the secret
of our Lord's whole life on earth that He set Himself to do
what God was doing—"to work the works of God."   As J. E.
Davey has clearly demonstrated in his recent book on the
Fourth Gospel, the doing of His Father's will was the guiding
principle of Jesus' life; He was "dependent upon the Father
at every point."[2] We must not think of "doing the Father's
will" as merely the language of mystical aspiration.   It was
in such practical things as healing a poor paralytic on the
Sabbath or speaking the truth in love to a disreputable
Samaritan woman beside a well that Jesus worked the works of
God.   It is a legitimate inference from what our Lord reveals of
His own mind in the Fourth Gospel that the question which
He asked was not so much; "What would my Father do in this
situation?" as "What is my Father doing through me here and
now?"   We might be truer to the mind of Christ if we did not
ask; "What would Jesus have done?" in complex modern
situations like a protest march about nuclear disarmament,
or a home where one partner persists in going into debt, or
even the rival claims on a Divinity student of academic study
and practical Christian service.   The Gospel accounts of
Jesus' activities provide no ready-made examples to follow
in such cases, and even indirect guidance is hard to discover.
Our business is to ask what God is doing through us here and
now, and—in a phrase of Brunner's—to let ourselves "be
placed within the activity of God."[3] Jesus' determination to
do His Father's will is an example that is relevant in every
situation; and it is to be remembered that God is at work in
the situations of our modern world, just as He was in the
situations of our Lord's life in Palestine, It is because we can
see His style of action in the life and work of Jesus that we can
discern His working in the world of today, and let ourselves
be placed within the plan of His activity.

    Christian theology has always had some difficulty in
maintaining that Jesus was truly man, and, at the same time,

------

[2] J. E. Davey, *The Jesus of St. John*, London 1958, p. 90.
[3] Brunner, *Divine Imperative*, p. 55.

in explaining why He did not share in some of the most characteristic of human experiences, the partnership of marriage, the upbringing of a family and, as far as we know, the earning of a living. (Our picture of Him supporting His mother and her family in Nazareth is a pious inference from Mark's single reference to him as "the carpenter"(Mk. vi.3), and can hardly be regarded as fundamental to the Gospel revelation.) If Jesus had shared these basic experiences, how useful, we are tempted to say, His example would have been. We cannot escape the difficulty by saying (what is perfectly true) that these things did not come into His particular vocation. The point is that the example He provided is not a detailed pattern for even the most universal human situations; it is an example of discerning and doing the will of God in any situation. Even then we must remember that His life was not only the perfect life of man, as God lived it; His life was also the revelation of God's action in relation to sinful men. Christ might have modified St Paul's words to make them; "Be ye imitators of me, as I am of God." Even in the earthly life of Christ, it is God Almighty who is our real example, and not a man limited by the relativities of our human conditions.

This discussion may throw a little light on two problems, the one of theology and the other of Biblical study. Many orthodox theologians have declared that the humanity of Christ was not that of an individual man, but that of mankind universally and inclusively. R. C. Moberley said; "He was not generically but inclusively man," and H. R. Mackintosh summed up the gist of this teaching (with which he was not in sympathy) in the words; "Because Christ as man is of universal and organic significance for mankind, it is not possible that He should be individual."[4] We can agree with Mackintosh that "the scholastic conception of the universal *humanitas* as itself real and concrete no longer satisfies the mind. . . . There is no such thing existing independently as *humanitas* or 'man in general'."[5] Yet Mackintosh saw that this doctrine has an ethical and spiritual significance, for example in "the wondrous combination in Christ of qualities which tend in other men

---

[4] H. R. Mackintosh, *The Person of Jesus Christ*, London 1912, p. 388.
[5] *Op. cit.*, p. 389.

to be only opposed angularities."[6] The very comprehensive-
ness of the moral qualities of Christ makes His example
for us in a particular situation difficult to discern. The
pattern He provides is a pattern for mankind as such without
particular reference to the common relativities of our human
situation, marriage, the rearing of children, wage-earning, and
the rest.

In our study of the Bible we find that very little is told in
the Gospels of what may be called without irreverence the
ordinary life of Jesus. Apart from one incident in the Temple,
which may be interpreted as indicating Jesus' difference from
His fellowmen because of His special relationship to the Father,
all that we know of the first thirty years of His life is His
obedience to His parents, His normal growth in body and mind,
His pleasing of God and man (Lk. ii.39-51) and His probable
occupation as a carpenter during part of this period (Mk. vi.3).
The narratives of His ministry, which may have lasted for
three or four years, emphasise His power as a miracle worker
and His authority as a teacher (things in which we do not
normally share), and picture a type of life and vocation which
were in many respects unique; the Christian religion has only
one Lord and Saviour. In these narratives there are certainly
incidents in which Christians from the Gospel-writers onwards
have seen Jesus to be our example. Such, for example, are
His washing of the disciples' feet (explicitly said to be an
example), His consideration for the hunger of the restored
daughter of Jairus, and His attitude to Mary's act of extravagant
generosity and to her critics. The devout reader of the Gospel
will always find an inspiration and example for his own way of
living in very different circumstances in such revealing glimpses
of our Lord's character as these. Yet the New Testament
gives us no detailed picture of our Lord's life, so that we could
model our own lives on His in the rather slavish way that a
young minister sometimes models himself on the older man
to whom he has been assistant; at one time the Church of
Scotland was threatened with a swarm of little George Macleods!
Yet no devout Christian would willingly part with what the
New Testament does tell us of our Lord's example. To
abandon the Gospel narratives as later and often mythical

---

[6] Mackintosh, *The Person of Jesus Christ*, p. 391.

constructions in the fashion of Bultmann and the more extravagant of the Form Criticism school is a grievous loss. For the
sake of the Christian ethic, if for no other reason, Christian
scholars must pursue the quest of the historical Jesus.

§ 3

It is a strange but significant fact that some of the New
Testament passages which most clearly enjoin the imitation of
Christ refer to something which seems quite beyond the range
of ordinary human morality—the self-emptying of Christ in
the Incarnation. The Christians in Philippi were not "of one
mind," and some thought that they were more in the right
than others probably in one of those petty disputes that still so
often disfigure the life of a Christian congregation. St Paul
does not quote a Gospel incident of a quarrel among disciples
and our Lord's dealing with it, as unfortunately he could have
done (e.g. Mk. x.41 f.); the example He gives is that of "Christ
Jesus, who, though he was in the form of God, did not count
equality with God a thing to be grasped, but emptied himself. . .
and became obedient unto death, even death on a cross" (Phil.
II.5-8). Here our example is not primarily that of the human
Jesus, but of the Second Person of the Trinity, Very God of
Very God. When St Paul in his practical way demanded a
good collection from the Corinthians on behalf of the "saints"
at Jerusalem, the Corinthians must have wondered why they
should put their hands so deep in their pockets to help Church
leaders who were often uncooperative and narrowly exclusive;
they must have felt as some of us Presbyterians would feel if
we were asked to give a collection on behalf of Anglican
bishops after one of their more ambiguous pronouncements on
the validity of our orders! St Paul in support of his plea
does not quote an instance of Jesus' generosity to such un-
neighbourly people (e.g. Lk. ix.49-56; cf. Lk. x.29-37); he
reminds the Corinthian Christians of what Christ had given
up in coming among men; "For you know the grace of our
Lord Jesus Christ, that though he was rich, yet for your sake
he became poor, so that by his poverty you might become
rich" (II Cor. viii.9).

Without this spirit, "the exactest imitation (of our Lord)

would only be lifeless unedifying mimicry. . . . Though echoed
to the letter . . . the soul of it would still be wanting, and would
no more be His example than a death-mask a living face."[7]
Like the holiness of God, the self-emptying of God in the
Incarnation and ultimately in the Atonement seems something
so much above us that it appears near to blasphemy to suggest
that we can imitate it; it would be so indeed, if it were not
God Himself Who promises His Spirit to His children. There
are both in the teaching and the example of Jesus vivid
illustrations of how this spirit works out in action. There is
the washing of the disciples' feet—a story with a preamble
telling of the Divine glory of Jesus and of His love to His
disciples (Jn. XIII.1-3). There is the silence of Jesus during
His trial—a complete absence of "reviling," in which St Peter
found an example and inspiration for the persecuted Christians
of North Asia Minor (1 Pet. II.23). There is the humble
submission to the burden of one's vocation in spite of the
weariness it brings, like the yoke under which the ox must
bend its head for its labours (Mt. XI.29). There is the call
to deny oneself with the ominous picture of the criminal
carrying his cross as Jesus Himself was to do later (Mk. VIII.34).
All this is very far from a casuistical deduction of rules or the
slavish imitation of a pattern, for it all depends, as St John
indicates, on the love of God being the source and inspiration
of our human love; this love of God is most clearly seen in the
self-sacrifice of the Cross (1 Jn. IV.9-11).

The example of God's self-denial and love in the coming
and crucifixion of Christ is something that is relevant in
every human situation and every human circumstance. John
Oman asks rhetorically about Jesus; "Was He interested in
art? Did He concern Himself about public service? Are we
in our complex time to have no other interests than sufficed
for His simpler age?"[8] The worth of each of these interests
must be considered on other grounds than the fact that Christ
apparently did not share them during His life on earth. To
say that we should not have them would be as stupid as to
say that we should have no children because Christ had none.
Yet the example of self-giving love is certainly relevant in

---

[7] J. Oman, *Grace and Personality*, Cambridge 1917, p. 238.
[8] *Op. cit.*, p. 239.

these interests. The artist who forgets himself in his art, the public servant who gives up his private ambitions for the service of the community, and even the ordinary parent who denies himself for the real, and not the worldly, good of his children, are, within their own limitations, following the example of Christ coming down in perfect love from Perfect Love for us men and our salvation.

In considering the present-day situation, Ellul says that the task of Christians, and especially of Christian laymen, is to "try to create a style of life which does not differentiate them from others, but yet permits them to escape from the stifling pressure of our present form of civilization."[9] One characteristic of this style of life should be the self-emptying love of which we have been speaking. It is a style of life that seems to many exceedingly difficult in the complex conditions of a capitalistic society, but it must have been just as difficult in an occupied country, seething with political discontents, in the time of Jesus. In our present circumstances the challenge of the Divine example comes in one special way. We have heard *ad nauseam* of the possibilities of doubling our standard of living in this scientific age, and whatever doubling the standard of living may mean, it certainly does not sound like self-emptying. For the moral challenge of our time is not our own material advancement but the fact that, with all our vaunted scientific progress, the greater part of the human race is under-fed, illiterate, and in dire poverty. "If any one has the world's goods and sees his brother in need, yet closes his heart against him, how does God's love abide in him?" (1 Jn. III.17). Should not God's self-giving in Christ be moving us to the emptying of ourselves by lowering our standard of living, so that both by public measures involving higher taxation and acts of private charity we should be doing more for our brethren in need, and especially for those refugees for whose conditions we are so directly responsible through the wars we have waged?

§ 4

What then of the sermons that have been preached on the

---

[9] J. Ellul, *The Presence of the Kingdom*, henceforth cited as *Presence*, London 1951, p. 59 f. Translation of *Présence au monde moderne*, Geneva 1948.

more detailed aspects of the life of Jesus as our example, of His obedience to Joseph and Mary as an example to our children, of His custom of attending the synagogue as an example of church-going, of His way of spending a Sabbath in Capernaum (a way not altogether in accordance with the rules of the Pharisees or even of some modern protagonists of the observance of the Lord's Day) as an example of our use of the Christian Sunday, of His rising early to pray as an example for the morning watch, or of His missionary methods as an example for modern evangelists? In so far as we can see His motives in these things, and especially as we can see them as expressions of the Divine self-giving, there is no doubt that they provide examples to us.

Yet our imitation must never be a slavish imitation. The minister who insisted on washing his elders' feet would lack, not only a sense of humour, but the Divine considerateness that would feel the embarrassment of these elders as acutely as our Lord felt Mary's embarrassment when she had done an unconventional action. This is not merely a question of different social customs. We need to remember that we are not like Christ, acting with God's full authority and completely free from sin in spite of temptation. For us to attempt to do just what Jesus did in every situation of life would be not only to forget our ignorance of much of Jesus' way of living (an ignorance for which we may not be responsible), but also to forget our own status as sinners relying on God's mercy alone. We need humility, common-sense, and humour in our copying of Christ; otherwise we shall follow the letter, of which we are told so little, and neglect the spirit, which is so fully revealed to us in the whole teaching of the New Testament.

Slavish imitation is not the best way of learning even from an ordinary teacher or from one to whom we give our hero-worship. The exchange of ideas, the challenge of actions that we in our circumstances may never be able to copy, the give and take of living together are among the many ways in which one human being can influence another for good. This is equally true of the grace of our Lord Jesus Christ, as we shall see in our next chapter. He comes to us not only as a pattern to copy, but as a companion to give strength, a leader to whom we can give our heart's loyalty, a Lord to be obeyed, and a

Saviour who has done for us what we cannot possibly do for ourselves.

There is a sense, too, in which Christ's challenge to us is a challenge to be ourselves, as He was Himself. Anything else might be in danger of encouraging that hypocrisy or play-acting which our Lord so frequently condemned.[10] To be oneself is, admittedly, not a principle emphasised in the New Testament; but we have indications of our Lord's recognition of individual differences in the nicknames He gave to His disciples. Peter was, like the other disciples, to follow Christ, but he was to be *petros*, the rock. James and John were, like the other disciples, to follow Christ, but Jesus saw them as "sons of thunder," and they were to be what sons of thunder become when transformed by Christ. It would be a denial of St Paul's whole concept of the glorious liberty of the sons of God, if the following of the example of Christ were a "lifeless, unedifying mimicry" of the human Jesus. He Himself startled people by His amazing originality, and by being so very different from the somewhat conventional religious leaders of His time. May not part of our imitation of Christ be to show something of the same originality in the very different circumstances of the twentieth century? That was how St Francis followed the example of Christ in the thirteenth century, and it may explain why he was so very different from Jesus.

Literature

H. R. MACKINTOSH, *The Person of Jesus Christ*, London 1912, pp. 383-406.
J. OMAN, *Grace and Personality*, Cambridge 1917, pp. 235-41.
C. H. DODD, *Gospel and Law*, Cambridge 1951, pp. 39-42.
J. E. DAVEY, *The Jesus of St. John*, London 1958.

[10] See Chapter VI.

Chapter IV

Grace and Goodness

IN his very great book *God was in Christ*, Donald Baillie wrote; "In a sense Christianity transcends morality altogether and there is no such thing as a Christian ethic."[1] Baillie was not at this point falling into the heresy of anti-nomianism and declaring that Christians can be indifferent about the kind of lives they live. What he meant was that the Christian Gospel of what God has done for us in Christ must always take precedence over and, indeed, be basic to anything that we are called to in Christian obedience. Even then, we find that, like St Paul, we do not do the good we want (Rom. VII.19), and our impotence drives us to despair, apart from what Christ has done for us. It is this impotence, so fully confirmed both by modern behaviouristic psychology and by experience of life without religion, that makes many people today very impatient with the counsels of the moralist, and very sceptical about the possibility of any moral improvement in the human race.

There are, however, dangers in this very proper subordination of ethics to theology. The ethical teaching of the Sermon on the Mount, with its emphasis on striving, ends with a parable which contrasts the stability of the man who "hears these words of mine and does them" with the utter ruin of the man who "hears these words of mine and does not do them" (Mt. VII.24-7). Christ's moral teachings do not only provide a portrait of perfection for Christians to contemplate, or a measuring-tape to assess the extent of their own shortcomings, or a moral code for a fully consummated Kingdom of God. They are commands of God, which men must endeavour to obey in a world where there are such familiar modern things

[1] D. M. Baillie, *God was in Christ*, London 1948, p. 115.

34

as forced labour, lustful looks, hypocrites making large dona-
tions to charity, and people worrying about how to get food and
clothes for their families. Certainly one function of this
"impossible ethic" is "to drive us away from ourselves to
God,"[2] not in the sense of minimising the importance of our
own conduct, but in the sense of realising that it is only with the
self denied and with God in us through Christ that the impossible ethic becomes possible. St Paul, the protagonist of
those who deny the possibility of a man saving himself by his
own efforts, is persistent in his exhortations to such high
efforts. "Be imitators of God" (Eph. v.1), "Abstain from
every form of evil" (1 Thess. v.22), "Work out your own
salvation with fear and trembling" (Phil. 11.12), are typical of
St Paul's general exhortations; but he also goes into the
detailed patterns of morality, in the home and family, in the
neighbourhood and state, within the Church and outside the
Church. In St Paul's own life there is evidence of intense
moral struggle. "Not that I have already obtained this or am
already perfect, but I press on to make it my own" (Phil.
III.12). "I pommel my body and subdue it, lest after preaching
to others I myself should be disqualified" (1 Cor. IX.27). There
is no lack of moral strenuousness here, and St Paul's moral
exhortations are not mere *parerga* to his theology; they are a
fundamental part of his Gospel.

Christians today are more likely to be influenced by a
scientific determinism which attributes all our misdemeanours
to our fixed human nature or our environmental conditions
than by a theological theory that leaves no room for human
effort because all that is good in man is the direct activity of
God. Both science and theology have their truths to teach;
the wise Christian tries to learn what science can tell him about
the springs of human action, and the humble Christian knows
that by himself he cannot do the good that he wishes to do.
Yet such knowledge was never intended to paralyse moral
effort. When Christian theology has tended to do so, Christians
have realised the danger of antinomianism, and have revised
their theology in the light of the Word of God. Today, when
behaviouristic psychology leads us in the same direction, it
may be that our psychological theories need also to be revised

[2] Baillie, *God was in Christ*, p. 116.

in the light of the personal dealings between God and man revealed in Holy Scripture.

On the other hand, Christian experience has found real danger in the whole-hearted pursuit of moral goodness. "Moralism" and "perfectionism" have become bad words in theological circles, and those who so regard them point a little unfairly to the Pharisees as shocking examples of people who concentrated on morals. Yet, as we shall see later, it was not the Pharisees' genuine moral effort that our Lord condemned. It is true that a morbid, introspective concentration on one's own moral or spiritual development leads to a self-centredness entirely opposed to our Lord's command to deny oneself. The man who strives for moral perfection is apt to take himself very seriously indeed, and the writings and prayers of such men, who were in other respects very great Christians, sometimes display a concentration on the self that would have been more fitting in one of the great Stoics than in a man who has denied himself and followed Christ. This, too, is a danger in the life of the enclosed religious orders. "To be a nun," says the Reverend Mother in a modern novel, "meant that one had chosen a life in which one was bound to do one's utmost to reach the highest possible perfection." This perfection was certainly sought for the sake of the world outside. "A convent of contemplatives was a spiritual power-house into which God's grace was drawn down and then distributed throughout the world in response to the prayers and sacrifices of those within."[3] This is the ideal of such a life, but this novel of Monica Baldwin's and her own autobiography[4] make it amply clear how few are called to this life of "heroic virtue," and how many perils beset one on the path to perfection. There is a paradox of self-denial; the more we strive to deny ourselves, the more we concentrate on ourselves, until we cry with St Paul; "Wretched man that I am! Who will deliver me from this body of death?" (Rom. VII.24).

Strenuous effort is not the only road to perfection. The lover will do, for the sake of his beloved, heroic deeds of self-sacrifice far beyond what he would accomplish in the pursuit

---

[3] M. Baldwin, *The Called and the Chosen*, London 1958, pp. 155, 219.
[4] M. Baldwin, *I Leap over the Wall*, London 1950.

of perfection, and Luther describes a stage in the Christian life when the Christian is "motivated purely by a sense of gratitude for the divine forgiveness."[5] For most of us this ecstatic experience is only attained in our highest moments, and the Christian life continues to be a pressing on to our goal. The New Testament has, however, other counsels for us than the injunction to sheer moral endeavour. (*a*) We ought to cultivate an interest in other people, which is something easier to practise in the open life of the world than in the enclosed life of a convent. "Let each of you look not only to his own interests, but also the interests of others" (Phil. II.4) was how St Paul put it just before he pointed to the example of the self-emptying of Christ. The failure of our imaginations to grasp the circumstances and attitudes of others is a stumbling-block in our own progress to goodness. (*b*) We ought to think of our actions as done for the glory of God. What the New Testament emphasises here is not a motive of esoteric devotion, but the simple fact that the good name of God is in the Christian's hands. "Let your light so shine before men," said our Lord, "that they may see your good works and give glory to your Father who is in heaven" (Mt. v.16). Even the Gentiles, seeing the good works of the Christians, will glorify God (Rom. xv.9). (*c*) The concentration of our minds on Christ as our example draws our minds away from ourselves. For St Paul, "it is no longer I who live, but Christ who lives in me" (Gal. II.20), and, however much more this may mean, it certainly means that where St Paul had at one time thought of himself, he now thinks of Christ. The moment of release from the paradox of self-denial was that in which St Paul realised that his moral struggle was Christ's struggle, and that Christ had already in fact won. (*d*) The Christian man has a vocation; he is "called to be an apostle" as well as to be a saint (Rom. I.I; I Cor. I.2), and the faithful carrying out of his vocation, as apostle or in any other God-given capacity, may bring interests and experiences which will transform his character without any thought being given to self-improvement.

We have said what must be said for the moral precepts of the New Testament and for moral endeavour in the Christian

---

[5] R. Niebuhr, *Christian Realism and Political Problems*, henceforth cited as *Christian Realism*, London 1954, p. 143.

life, and yet we must frankly admit that these things are not
at the heart of the Christian Gospel even in its concern for
moral goodness. The alternative might appear to be that the
Christian's efforts should be concentrated on cultivating a
state of passivity, or waiting upon God, so that He may act,
not only for us and on us, but in us. There is certainly a place
for this attitude in the Christian life, and it is what gives ethical
significance to many of the practices of Christian worship.
But it is the peculiar temptation of the devout that this waiting
upon God becomes the sole concern of their religion, and thus
they may ignore the whole New Testament teaching on
practical conduct and service. What God gives us in waiting
upon Him is usually not only a gift but a task—a spiritual
work within us, which is at the same time a challenge to
decision and action. This action, as Brunner points out, takes
the distinctively ethical form of service to our fellowmen, for
"God does not wish us to offer Him any special sacrifice,
intended for Himself alone."[6]

§ 2

The way in which God participates in, and indeed takes
possession of, our moral endeavour is called, in the New
Testament, grace. Grace transcends the sphere of morality,
and indeed includes all that God has done for us in creation
and more especially in redemption. Grace more than com-
prehends the justice, the steadfast love, and the faithfulness
of God revealed in the Old Testament. All God's gifts to us,
food and clothing, health and strength, the beauty and mystery
of the universe, our human endowments and talents are the
lesser gifts of God's grace, but the gifts that chiefly concern
us here are those gifts that have a more direct power to transform us and our actions—the gifts given through the mighty
acts of God in Jesus Christ.

We must, however, avoid an over-narrow view of the
grace of God suggested by the teachings of some Roman
sacramentarians and even some Protestant theologians, namely
that grace is a kind of injection of mysterious power giving to

----

[6] Brunner, *Divine Imperative*, p. 189.

its recipient a disposition towards goodness, and an additional strength in the spiritual struggle against evil,—doing for the soul very much what the secretions from the adrenal glands do for the body in a physical struggle. In Romanist thought, God does this in quite a special way through the sacraments; in Protestant thought, He does it more generally and more arbitrarily to the elect. We need not deny that God sometimes does His work of grace, either in the sacraments or elsewhere, in as mysterious and even miraculous a way as those our Lord used in His miracles of healing. The saints have borne a continuing testimony to such apparently miraculous accessions of strength granted in their moral struggles. Yet there is nothing in the New Testament to limit the gift of grace to such experiences.

What must be avoided here is any thought that God's grace forces us, even against our wills, to do what is right, what John Oman described magnificently as "the irresistible force of omnipotence directed in an unswerving line by omniscience"[7] In whatever way grace comes to us, it does not interfere with our human freedom of choice. The modern world has long rejected the view that human rulers should force their subjects to do what the rulers believe to be God's will for them. God certainly never forces men to do His will; He does not even bribe men to do it, as Utilitarian moralists sometimes expect Him to do. "He makes his sun rise on the evil and on the good, and sends rain on the just and on the unjust" (Mt. v.45). Our danger today, however, is not so much the tendency to expect God to provide inducements to good conduct, as to regard our circumstances as affording all the guidance that we can expect, and so to let them lead us along the line of least resistance. Circumstances are not irresistible forces driving us to particular actions; they may be obstacles to be overthrown rather than conditions determining our actions. In the life stories of many great missionaries, almost insuperable difficulties were put in the way of their missionary vocation. Gladys Aylward, the heroine of *The Inn of the Sixth Happiness*, is not the only great missionary to be rejected as unsuitable by a missionary society, and yet to find her own way to her God-given vocation. We need to remember today, both in

[7] Oman, *Grace and Personality*, p. 10.

D

formal education and in the Christian discipline of life, that it is part of our Christian duty "to breast the blows of circumstance."

The grace of God is not a matter of irresistible force but a matter of personal encounter. God, as Person, deals with men as persons. The nearest, although still quite inadequate, analogies of God's dealings in grace with men are a wise parent's dealings with his children or a wise schoolmaster's dealings with his pupils. There is a place for direct commands and prohibitions, and the disobeying of them must produce consequences that teach a lesson, but this kind of thing does not loom too large in a good family or a good school. There is the suggestion given both by word and by example, and this is probably most effective when it is least obvious. There are the opportunities offered, again not too obviously by the wisest parents and teachers, for young people to do and discover things for themselves, and especially for serving others. There are hard tasks to be done, but these are not so hard when the child discovers through them the ready co-operation and understanding of parent or teacher and the strength that comes from fellowship. There is the security which children find in the love of others, and in which they can let themselves go freely in creative activity. There is the growth in wisdom and goodness which comes unconsciously through daily intercourse with the experienced and the good. Those who have had a really great teacher know that what mattered in him was not the knowledge he imparted but that indefinable something which he gave us, we know not how. The good parent or the good teacher never asserts his own personality too obviously; otherwise we call him dominating and expect ill effects in the child he is bringing up. We have been describing what a good parent or teacher does for his children, but of course we have been thinking of what God does for us by His grace. All this has been expressed in very different language by a great Scottish theologian of the last generation, John Oman, who stood for the sanctity of human personality even in its encounter with Almighty God. In Oman's writings, one seems to hear God's challenge to Ezekiel; "Stand upon your feet, and I will speak with you" (Ezek. II.1). God deals with us as men and He has as little use as we have for an insincere obsequiousness or a cringing self-abasement such as St Paul found in the Colossian heretics.

While it is impossible to overemphasise the personal nature of God's dealings with us in grace, this is not the whole story. God is God, and not man, personal, yet more than a person, and as transcendent Being He has ways of bestowing grace to which we do not find analogies in gracious human relationships. We have spoken of the sacraments, and we can well understand by such analogies as a gift of flowers or the marriage ring how the sacraments "signify and seal" what God has done and is doing for us. The heart of the sacrament is, however, God's mysterious work within us, and for that there is no adequate human analogy. There is, again, God's gracious action in the experience of the mystic, something experienced only by a few Christians, just as by a few in the other great religions. Not even the union of man and woman is adequate analogy for the mystical union of the soul with Christ, although it is the one most frequently used. This mystical experience has the danger of obscuring the moral responsibility of man in the presence of a personal God, which is fundamental to Biblical religion and to the Christian ethic. The experience of mystical union is, perhaps, to be regarded as a *charisma*—a special gift of the Holy Spirit, like "speaking with tongues," that is given to few people. Our exaltation of it and our tendency to identify it with Christian love may have come from the *eros* philosophy of the Greeks rather than the religion of the Bible.

There is an action of the grace of God that is mediated through other human beings. David Cairns describes in his autobiography, how, as he looked at his dead father "it suddenly flashed upon me what a living message from God Himself he had been to me all my days, of far more real meaning to a free human spirit than any articulate thunder could have been, even though it spoke my name. After all, a human being is a far richer means of Divine expression than any natural thing or force could possibly be. Here from my earliest childhood had been one beside me influencing me in a thousand gentle ways in favour of uprightness, kindness, unselfishness and faith, making it easier at every stage for me to believe in goodness and in God. God Himself had all my life through my father been telling me how He felt towards me and how He would have me think and act."[8]   St Teresa probably went too far when she said; "Christ has no body on earth but yours," for God speaks to us and acts on us in other ways than through His servants.   He speaks to us through the works of nature and in the deep places of the heart.

The grace of God is not only God's providential dealing with us here and now, however widely that is conceived.   The grace of God, as it is revealed in the New Testament and as it most directly concerns the good life, is bound up with certain events that happened at the beginning of the Christian era— the incarnation, ministry, death, and resurrection of Jesus and His giving of the Holy Spirit.   It is not merely the fact that the life and teachings of Jesus still influence our life and conduct in the way that the life and teachings of Socrates still influence many people.   The Holy Spirit makes what happened then immediately and directly relevant to our lives here and now.   Theologians in their various theories of the atonement go some way in explaining the relevance of these events to our justification;   they are less successful so far in explaining their relevance to our sanctification, which is the more special concern of Christian ethics.   "He died to make us good," but just how does His death make us good?   The work of the Special Commission on Baptism of the Church of Scotland is of special interest here with its emphasis on the living power of these events not only in the sacrament of Baptism, but in the whole of the Christian life that continues from Baptism to the resurrection of the body.

§ 3

We can now see more clearly why moralism has such a bad reputation.   While theologians fulminate with St Paul and Luther against the doctrine of justification by works, ordinary people cling tenaciously to this most common of Christian heresies.   When an ordinary man says of another; "He is a real Christian," he commonly means that this man is justified by his works.   Most Christian ministers have had sad experience of people who refuse to be elders or even communicant

[8] D. S. Cairns, *David Cairns: an autobiography*, London 1950, p. 48.

members, because, as they say, they are "not good enough" to
take the step. One of our hardest tasks is to rid men's minds of
this false belief, without weakening the other side of our message
that men are called to be saints in the most practical ways of
living. Even St Paul sometimes seems to have found it difficult
to integrate completely his proclamation of the Gospel with
his moral exhortations, so that in some of his letters there is
too marked a division between the two parts. St John was
more successful in his first epistle, and it is still by proclaiming
the love of God as the source of our human love one to the other
that we can make our theology most obviously relevant to our
ethical teaching.

Moralism is wrong in giving too large a place to praise and
blame. The Pharisees found it difficult not to think of the
privileges of the Jews as earned, if not by their own good works
at least by the merits of the patriarchs. St Paul saw quite
clearly that Jews and Gentiles were equally undeserving;
"all have sinned and fall short of the glory of God" (Rom.
III.23). There is certainly no room for praise of ourselves;
whatever is good in us is the work of God's grace, and that is
true of others as well as ourselves. When it comes to blame,
again we are not to judge others (Mt. VII.1); our judgments
would take no proper account of the circumstances in which
others find themselves, and so judgment on them must be
left to the final judgment of God. Yet there is one person
whom we are bidden to judge—our own self. "If we judged
ourselves truly we should not be judged" (I Cor. XI.31). It is
easy to think of our modern tolerance of evil as a Christian
thing obeying Christ's command not to judge others, and
making charitable allowance for the circumstances of our
neighbour. It can only be a Christian thing if it is accompanied
by a full realisation of our own sin and guilt. Without this,
Christian charity can easily lead to the moral indifference that
is so common today.

An even more subtle form of moralism is to regard our
faith as a qualification for receiving the grace of God. The
evangelical Christian, realising that a man cannot be justified
by his moral actions, substitutes for them an inner moral condition which he calls faith. It is because a sinner lacks faith
that he does not receive the blessings of the Gospel. More

cruelly, it is even suggested that a sick man misses Christ's healing because he lacks faith. Faith is not a moral virtue; it is the seeing that God is faithful, worthy of the trust of altogether unworthy people. Our faith in Sir Winston Churchill as a war leader indicated no virtue in us; it was his quality of reliability and perseverance that was the virtue. To quote John Oman again; "We are justified by faith, because faith is a discernment of God's mind, and not because it is a specially meritorious state of our minds."[9]

The task of the preacher of the Gospel is to set forth the facts through which the plain man may discern God's mind and so have faith in Him. That discernment includes the realisation that God makes moral demands on His people; Christ never cancelled these demands. It includes also the realisation that it is only in a living incorporation in the Christ who Himself fulfilled these demands that we can in any sense fulfil them. We lose ourselves in His righteousness in justification, and we find His righteousness transforming us in sanctification.

Literature

J. OMAN, *Grace and Personality*, Cambridge 1917.
D. M. BAILLIE, *God was in Christ*, London 1948, pp. 106-32 and *passim*.
P. S. WATSON, *The Concept of Grace*, London 1959.

[9] Oman, *Grace and Personality*, p. 194.

Chapter V

Conscience in the New Testament

THE word "conscience" does not have the same meaning in the New Testament as it has in either ordinary or more technically ethical usage in modern English. Conscience, according to one definition in the *Shorter Oxford English Dictionary*, is "the faculty or principle which pronounces upon the moral quality of one's actions or motives, approving the right and condemning the wrong." It is this function of pronouncing judgment that English usage emphasises. Milton spoke of "my umpire conscience."[1] Butler preached; "This faculty [of conscience] was placed within to be our proper governor," and; "You cannot form a notion of this faculty, conscience, without taking in judgment, direction, superintendency. This is a constituent part of the idea, that is, of the faculty itself: and, to preside and govern, from the very economy and constitution of man, belongs to it."[2] Kant was equally clear; "Conscience is an instinct to pass judgment upon ourselves in accordance with moral laws. . . . Its judgment is not logical but judicial."[3] Butler held that "conscience is assigned to us by the author of our nature,"[4] and Kant believed that the conscience of a man must regard God as the judge of his actions,[5] although neither would go so far as to say with Menander; "To every man his own conscience is God,"[6] or with Newman; "Conscience is the aboriginal Vicar of Christ."[7]

[1] J. Milton, *Paradise Lost*, III.195.
[2] J. Butler, *Fifteen Sermons preached at the Rolls Chapel*, henceforth cited as *Sermons*, in Butler's *Works*, ed. W. E. Gladstone London 1896. VOL. II, p. 64.
[3] Kant, *Lectures on Ethics*, p. 129.
[4] Butler, *Sermons*, VOL. II, p. 71.
[5] I. Kant, *Tugendlehre*, p. 293, quoted in *Critique of Practical Reason*, trans. by T. K. Abbott, 3rd edn., London 1883, p. 322.
[6] Quoted Dodd, *Gospel and Law*, p. 70.
[7] J. H. Newman, *A Letter addressed to His Grace the Duke of Norfolk*, London 1875, p. 57.

However often it may have been preached from pulpits, this is not the teaching of the New Testament about conscience.

C. A. Pierce, whose monograph, *Conscience in the New Testament* is the basis of much of this chapter, says that συνείδησις, the New Testament word translated "conscience," meant in ordinary Greek speech "the pain suffered by man, as man . . . when, by his acts completed or initiated, he transgresses the moral limits of his nature."[8]   What the New Testament emphasises is the painfulness of conscience—"the painful consciousness that a man has of his own sins, past or, if present, begun in the past,"[9] rather than the pronouncing of judgment or the providing of guidance for the future.   Yet we cannot separate entirely the two usages; the painful reaction of a man's nature against his past sins is likely to be expressed in an adverse judgment on these sins, which will serve as an authoritative guidance to avoid them in future.

There is at first sight no obvious Old Testament term corresponding to "conscience," but this may be due to the act that the Hebrew language does not reflect a "faculty psychology" in the way that the English language does.   The fact of conscience—the pain suffered after committing an action recognised to be wrong—was something experienced by the Hebrews as by mankind generally.   It is expressed by the phrase; "David's heart smote him" (1 Sam. xxiv.5), and negatively by Job; "My heart does not reproach me for any of my days" (Job xxvii.6).   Indeed the word "heart" (*leb*) is often almost equivalent to our English "conscience;"[10] in particular the Old Testament "integrity of heart" is close to the New Testament "clear conscience" (Gen. xx.5, 6; 1 Kings ix.4, etc.).   In the Greek Wisdom of Solomon, a book in which Hellenistic influences are apparent, συνείδησις is used with its ordinary meaning; "Wickedness . . . being pressed hard by conscience, always forecasteth the worst lot" (Wis. xvii.11).

It is to the Greek tradition that we must chiefly look for the history of the word.   The common opinion that συνείδησις was primarily a philosophical term used by the Stoics has been

---

[8] C. A. Pierce, *Conscience in the New Testament*, henceforth cited as *Conscience in N.T.*, Studies in Biblical Theology vol. xv, London 1955, p. 54.

[9] *Op. cit.*, p. 111.

[10] E.g. Deut. ix.5; 1 Kings iii.6; Ps. cxix.7.

finally disproved by H. Osborne[11] and Pierce, who shows that of the eighty-nine occurrences of συνείδησις and its cognates in classical and Hellenistic secular literature, only three are from Stoic philosophers, one with the wide non-moral meaning of "consciousness" and the other two belonging to a generation later than that of St Paul. It may be that συνείδησις was a much older philosophical term that had come to be used loosely in common speech, but it is even more likely that it was originally a vague word in common use which was taken up later by St Paul and other intellectuals. Like our English "conscience" in earlier times, συνείδησις had both a non-moral use denoting something like "consciousness," which Pierce finds three times in the New Testament (II Cor. iv.2, v.11; I Pet. ii.19), and the moral use with which we are concerned here. In secular Greek literature συνείδησις is concerned with a man's own actions, and not with the actions of other people. They are normally past actions, or actions already begun, and they are usually bad actions, so that conscience is normally painful. If "conscience" does not indicate "a bad conscience," there is a qualifying adjective like "good" or "clean." As we might expect of a word in popular use, it is not clear whether conscience is itself the pain, or the inflictor of the pain or the faculty that feels the pain. Pierce finds that the word is used in the New Testament very much as it is used in other literature. Of the thirty-one occurrences of συνείδησις and its immediate cognates in the New Testament, sixteen refer clearly to a bad conscience, and in nine others there is the same implication negatively—there is nothing on one's conscience. There are indications, however, that the notion is developing somewhat in the modern direction, as in II Cor. i.12; "The testimony of our conscience [is] that we have behaved . . . with holiness and godly sincerity."

It certainly looks as if moralists have given "conscience" a meaning and place that the New Testament does not give it. Of course, conscience is something with which our Christian religion is concerned; the thirty-one occurrences of συνείδησις in the New Testament confirm this; but there is little to suggest that conscience is "our proper governor," still less "the

---

[11] H. Osborne, Συνείδησις in *Journal of Theological Studies*, xxxii (1931), pp. 167-79.

aboriginal Vicar of Christ." The Word of God, however spoken, has alone the authority for Christians which many have given to conscience. Conscience is, as Butler rightly demonstrated, something given in our human nature, from which the Christian like everyone else can obtain guidance. It may be true, as Pierce puts it, that "where there is conscience the choice was wrong, the action must be abandoned and the choice revised,"[12] although it is doubtful whether this can be maintained if we admit that conscience is not the ultimate criterion. The man in whom the use of contraceptives causes pains of conscience is probably right to accept the guidance of conscience for himself. What is certainly wrong is that we should try to prevent the use of contraceptives by others, because the whole idea rouses in us a feeling of repugnance very similar to the pains of conscience. The wider moral question must be decided on grounds other than our feelings even although we label them "conscience." In any case conscience can be corrupted and misled. "I beseech you, in the bowels of Christ," wrote Cromwell to the General Assembly of the Church of Scotland, "think it possible you may be mistaken."[13]

§ 2

The phrase, "for conscience' sake," which translates διὰ τὴν συνείδησιν three times in the Authorised Version, suggests, on the analogy of the familiar "for Jesus' sake," the high authority and regard commonly given to conscience. In Rom. xiii.5 submission to the civil magistrate is enjoined "not only to avoid God's wrath but also for the sake of conscience." The same preposition, διὰ, is translated "to avoid" in the first clause and "for the sake of" in the second. This appears inconsistent, and διὰ, which normally means "on account of" may be interpreted, as by Pierce, "to avoid" in both clauses. This throws a new light on the modern opinion that conscience is a valid reason for disobeying the orders of a government, as in the case of the conscientious objector. St Paul expects that the man who thus resists the authority of the state should, on

---

[12] Pierce, *Conscience in N.T.*, p. 127.
[13] T. Carlyle, *Oliver Cromwell's Letters and Speeches*, 5 vols., London 1871. VOL. III, p. 18.

the one hand, suffer the "wrath of God" executed by the sword
of the magistrate and, on the other, pains of conscience. The
man who finds in God's Word or in the leading of the Holy
Spirit warrant to disobey the law of the state must expect the
physical punishments that the state imposes, and the New
Testament never suggests that he should be exempted from
them as a matter of right. He may also expect the pains of
conscience, and it is a fact that the more sensitive conscientious
objector has always found his decision not to identify himself
with his Christian fellow countrymen in the war effort a
cause of deep heart-searching and pain. We should not now-
adays call this particular pain "conscience," but perhaps St
Paul would have done so. If the conscientious objector should
not be diverted from what he believes to be the will of God
for him by this particular pain, it seems likely that the similar
pain of conscience does not provide a final criterion for what
is right. The situation of breaking the law for conscience' sake
is certainly a great deal more complicated than some simple-
minded pacifists find it to be.

In 1 Cor. x the Corinthians are told not to ask questions
as to the source of meat sold in the shops or provided at a
non-Christian neighbour's table "for conscience' sake." The
knowledge that the meat had been previously offered to an
idol might cause the eater or even a spectator pains of conscience: "for conscience' sake" here too seems to mean "to
avoid the pains of conscience." If, however, one is explicitly
told that the meat has been offered to an idol, then out of
consideration for the person giving the information (presumably
a scrupulous Christian) and for the sake of *his* conscience one
must not eat it. This contradicts a common idea that conscience provides a kind of esoteric guidance as to what is
wrong, for it is only when a man has learned by chance that
the meat has been defiled that conscience is roused at all.
Conscience is relative to knowledge. This passage also
indicates that it is a definite Christian duty to avoid causing
other people pains of conscience. St Paul had little use for
the man who sticks to his own principles without any consideration of the pain caused to others by their being carried out.
One wonders whether the ardent believer in Sunday games
and the equally ardent upholder of Sabbath observance laws

have not both something to learn from St Paul here. The young minister certainly should keep this in mind when he wishes to introduce thoroughly desirable innovations in a conservatively-minded congregation.

The phrase διὰ συνείδησιν also occurs in 1 Pet. II.19 in the clause translated literally; "If on account of conscience of God one endures pain, suffering unjustly." Conscience is here given a non-moral meaning by most interpreters; the Revised Standard Version begins the clause; "If mindful of God." Yet the reference to pain in the context suggests the possibility of a moral interpretation as in Rom. XIII.5., where the pains of conscience are to be avoided like God's wrath. The unjustly persecuted man, like the man who resists the authority of the state, may sometimes be afflicted with painful doubts; "Can I be wrong after all?" On this moral interpretation, "God's conscience" could only mean conscience implanted by God, and we must admit that it seems scarcely likely that St Peter would attribute what looks like an undesirable manifestation of conscience to God's implanting.

"For conscience' sake" in the New Testament never implies that conscience is the voice of God demanding obedience. The pains of conscience are to be avoided not only by scrupulous attention to right conduct, but also by such indirect methods as refraining from asking unnecessary questions and accepting, where other considerations permit, the standards of the civil authority. St Paul certainly did not regard "conscientiousness" in the sense of deliberately cultivating the pains of conscience as a virtue.

§ 3

While dealing with this same matter of the eating of sacrificial meats in 1 Cor. VIII, St Paul refers thrice to "weak consciences" and twice to "weak" people. The man of weak conscience is here the man who still thinks of the idol as having power to defile the food offered to it, but who is in such a state of uncertainty about the whole business that he follows the example of a "man of knowledge" who does not share his scruples, eats the meat, and so suffers the pains of conscience. St Paul's phrase; "Their conscience is defiled," expresses graphically what a man of this kind would himself feel after eating the food.

This man is not weak in the sense that his conscience is insensitive; his conscience is, if anything, over-sensitive. He is weak in the sense that he has no firm principles on the matter; he is not, as St Paul says in the same connexion elsewhere, "fully convinced in his own mind" (Rom. xiv.5), as a mature Christian ought to be; otherwise he would not have followed the example of the man of knowledge. St Paul does not despise such men; they are the brothers for whom Christ died; yet he frankly recognises their limitations. It is the superstition remaining from their former heathenism which causes them to feel pangs of conscience after eating meat offered to idols, and it is insufficient knowledge of Christian doctrine that makes them be led so easily by the example of a man of knowledge.

This weak man's conscience clearly does not provide him with final authoritative guidance. His state is still that of the heathen, described in Rom. ii.15; "What the law requires is written on their hearts, while their conscience also bears witness and their conflicting thoughts accuse or perhaps excuse them." This, as we have already seen, is a difficult passage, but it does indicate that even for the heathen conscience does not have the final word; otherwise how could there be alongside of it conflicting thoughts or arguments? St Paul's chief concern in 1 Cor. viii, as in 1 Cor. x, is not that a man should be guided by his conscience, but that nothing should be done to aggravate the pains of conscience of the weaker brother. To sin against one's brothers in this way is to sin against Christ.

Conscience can be corrupted so that it may feel no pain after wrong actions are committed, or, less commonly, so that it may feel pain after right actions are done. The New Testament does not directly mention the fact, obvious to all moralists, that the habitual disregard of the pains of conscience leads to the deadening of these pains. (It does suggest that this happens to the voice of the Holy Spirit, 1 Thess. v.19.) What the New Testament does emphasise is the corruption of conscience caused by false doctrine (1 Tim. iv.2; Tit. 1.15). This is probably the chief factor in the corruption of men's consciences at the present time. Ignorance of the fundamental doctrines of the Christian faith and an unthinking acceptance of the teachings of certain schools of modern psychology, positivist philosophy, and scientific materialism, as they are mediated by the popular newspapers and the radio, may so corrupt men's consciences that they see nothing wrong in things that are really evil, and feel no pain of conscience after their own wicked actions. Butler and Kant and Newman could give an unscriptural authority to conscience, because they had in view consciences for long educated and enlightened by a Christian tradition of sound doctrine. The New Testament writers and we in the twentieth century are unfortunately more familiar with consciences seared by the false doctrine of those who, "giving heed to commands of men, reject the truth" (Tit 1.14).

In 1 Cor. VIII St Paul goes a step further. Through the knowledge of the more sophisticated Christian (and St Paul does not deny that it may be true knowledge), who wittingly or unwittingly leads a weaker brother to do things that cause him pains of conscience, "this weak man is destroyed." Some have interpreted this as suggesting that to act against one's conscience is the unforgivable sin. It is more likely that St Paul is pointing to the fact that the weak man so misled becomes what we should call a disintegrated personality. The modern psychiatrist does not speak of men being destroyed by acting against their consciences, but he does attribute many harmful neuroses to a conflict very like that which St Paul saw in the man of weak conscience. Bonhoeffer says similarly that "disregard for the call of conscience will necessarily entail the destruction of one's own being."[14]

Here is one application of the teaching of 1 Cor. VIII. We in the Churches which practise more open Communion would claim to be "men of knowledge" in this matter, and consider that the Anglican insistence that the elements be administered by an episcopally ordained minister is the kind of superstition that St Paul's "weaker brother" might have shared. Whether we are right or wrong is not the chief Christian consideration. The important thing is that the taking of the elements from a priest not episcopally ordained would certainly cause pains

[14] D. Bonhoeffer, *Ethics*, London 1955, p. 211. Translation of *Ethik*, Munich 1949.

of conscience to many devout Anglicans, and so the demand that they should do so as a preliminary to any union negotiations is an un-Christian demand. Consideration for the scruples of other Christians is a primary Christian duty, and may in the long run be more effective in breaking down these scruples than demands for precipitate action or prolonged theological discussion.

§ 4

In those New Testament writings which are influenced, if not written by St Paul—the Pastoral Epistles, Hebrews, Acts, and I Peter, there are references to a good conscience ($\dot{\alpha}\gamma\alpha\theta\dot{\eta}$, I Tim. 1.5, 19; Acts XXIII.1; I Pet. III.16, 21; $\kappa\alpha\lambda\dot{\eta}$, Heb. XIII.18), a clear conscience ($\kappa\alpha\theta\alpha\rho\dot{\alpha}$, I Tim. III.9; II Tim. 1.3), and a pure conscience ($\dot{\alpha}\pi\rho\dot{\sigma}\kappa\sigma\pi\sigma\varsigma$, Acts XXIV.16); it looks as if the use of the term "conscience" is developing. A good conscience is the conscience of a man like St Paul, who can look back and claim that he has not done anything which has caused him pains of conscience. The possession of such a good conscience does not mean that he has not sinned. "I am not aware of anything ($\sigma\dot{\nu}\nu\sigma\iota\delta\alpha$) against myself," St Paul wrote, "but I am not thereby acquitted; it is the Lord who judges me" (I Cor. IV.4). Once again conscience does not provide a final standard; that is given only by the judgment of God.

According to Pierce, the writer to the Hebrews shows "that the Christian life moves steadily away from the pain of conscience. . . . The Christian, as he grows, may hope that its place may be taken more and more by joy."[15] As a Christian is freed from his sins, he is also freed from the pains of conscience, and no other method, whether the performance of ritual acts or moral effort, can give these freedoms in the way that the salvation offered in the Gospel does. Yet it is commonly believed that an increased sensitivity to the pains of conscience is a sign of spiritual growth. The man who in his unregenerate days suffered conscience only when he committed adultery now feels remorse after a lustful thought; the man who used every loop-hole in the rules to avoid with a good conscience the payment of income tax, now feels pain and pays "conscience money." There is Scriptural warrant for such a

[15] Pierce, *Conscience in N.T.*, p. 102.

development in the encounter of Zacchaeus with Christ. There is, however, another side to this, and Christians who ignore it are fairly charged with morbidity about sin. The Christian who casts all his anxious care on Christ should include his pains of conscience in that anxious care. There is need of intellectual honesty here. In our modern pastoral theology, we are all out to get rid of complexes, conflicts, neuroses, and the like in ourselves and others, but, when we preach our traditional Christian doctrine, we tend to hold on to these things under older, hallowed names. The New Testament values as highly as modern psychiatry a "clear conscience toward God and toward men" (Acts xxiv.16), and this may suggest that the committed Christian should be less preoccupied with his own sins than some very saintly Christians have been. Yet the whole matter is complicated by the fact that a man with no pain of conscience is much more likely to be a hardened sinner with his conscience seared than a saint with a genuinely clear conscience.

§ 5

Our attention to the single term συνείδησις with its painful connotation must not blind us to the fact that the New Testament is concerned with the whole man and not with one particular faculty. Even the pagan appears to have a more positive guide to right action than the pains of conscience, although the *daemon* of Socrates also only gave him negative guidance. The pagan has some kind of law written on his heart (Rom. ii.15), and the power of reading it, whether or not we call that power "conscience" as many do.

The Holy Spirit, whom Jesus promised to guide His disciples into all the truth (Jn. xvi.13), certainly gives them moral guidance. Indeed He does the work of conscience more adequately, even as we have conceived it negatively; "He will convince the world of sin and of righteousness and of judgment" (Jn. xvi.8-11). The primary work of the Holy Spirit, which is His testifying to Christ, results among other things in those who receive Him being convinced of their own sinfulness. The guidance of the Holy Spirit is never merely moral; it is a religious Christ-centred guidance. This is indicated in the interpretation of the convincing that we have just mentioned—"of sin, because they do not believe in me; of righteousness because I go to the Father; . . . of judgment, because the ruler of this world is judged." We may regard the Holy Spirit as the enlightener of conscience—a function suggested by St Paul's phrase; "My conscience bears me witness in the Holy Spirit" (Rom. ix.1). If conscience is conditioned by environment and habit—a fact of psychology which St Paul accepts in his discussion of the weak conscience—it must also be conditioned by the Christian Gospel, which is brought home to men's hearts by the Holy Spirit.

Modern psychologists, at least in the psycho-analytical schools, tend to neglect the purely intellectual elements in conscience to which Butler and Kant gave so much attention. In their analysis of conscience in terms of the super-ego,[16] they do, however, find some elements which are implied in the New Testament teaching as well as other more debatable elements; their language, of course, is very different from that of the New Testament. They hold, for example, that conscience is in part conditioned by environment, drawing particular attention to the individual's tendency to incorporate in his super-ego the precepts and moral attitudes of others, especially his own parents—a view that St Paul would certainly have accepted. They make much also of the pain of conscience, which has figured so largely in our study of conscience in the New Testament, tracing it back to the tendency to turn one's aggressive instincts against the self and the subconscious desire to inflict pain on the self in ways that the New Testament did not consider. What is most significant, however, is that much of the practice of psycho-analysis is directed to the avoiding of undesirable pains of conscience, an object of which St Paul would have approved. Less than justice, however, is done to the more valuable and positive aspects of conscience, which the Christian tradition has so strongly emphasised.

Conscience is not enough. Whether we interpret it in terms of consequent pain, as in the New Testament, or in terms of an intuitive faculty, as in the work of the eighteenth-century English moralists, or in terms of the super-ego it does not do justice to the full range of Christian moral experience.

[16] See e.g. J. C. Flugel, *Man, Morals and Society*, London 1945.

E

It is easy to make the voice or pains of conscience the arbiter in a situation which demands thought and prayer and a deep searching of the Scriptures in order to discover God's will, and its decisions may be prejudiced by past disobedience or false doctrine or a hundred other things of which we are quite unconscious. The wise Christian will give due weight to conscience; it is the natural reaction of his whole being as it has been developed under Christian influences. He will realise that by disobeying conscience he may be in danger of destroying himself. Yet he will turn more confidently to other more objective and more reliable standards, which he can fully and reasonably accept as his own,—the Word of God and the example of Christ and even the Natural Law known and approved by all reasonable men. For a Christian man's conscience, in so far as it is really Christian, has been taught by these standards.

Literature

C. A. PIERCE, *Conscience in the New Testament*, Studies in Biblical Theology VOL. XV, London 1955.

J. P. THORNTON-DUESBERY, "Conscience," in *A Theological Word Book of the Bible*, ed. A. Richardson, London 1950, p. 52f.

J. BUTLER, *Fifteen Sermons preached at the Rolls Chapel*, in *Works*, ed. W. E. Gladstone, London 1896, VOL. II, Sermons II and III.

H. OSBORNE, "Συνείδησις" in *Journal of Theological Studies*, XXXII (1931), pp. 167-79.

C. SPICQ, "La Conscience dans le Nouveau Testament," in *Revue biblique*, XLVII (1938), pp. 50-80.

Chapter VI

Goodness and Knowledge

IN this age of self-criticism the Christian minister and the Christian teacher are haunted by the question; "Can knowledge make men good?" The ancient Greeks had no doubt about the answer; the master Socrates had taught that virtue is knowledge and even older moralists had found the secret of right living in the maxim, "Know thyself." One of the assumptions of modern thought also is that improved education and improved environment, both of which appear attainable by the techniques of science, will produce better men and women. In recent years much public money has been poured into better equipped and more adequately staffed schools, and the cynic may say that the most obvious result has been an increase in juvenile delinquency. Christians share, with some hesitations, the prevailing view. We teach our children in Sunday Schools, hoping that they will become better as well as more knowledgeable children, and some of us imagine that we are better men today because we learned the Shorter Catechism by heart when we were children. Yet our Lord gave thanks that these things had been hidden from the wise and understanding and revealed to babes (Mt. xi.25, 26). It is time that we considered what the New Testament has to say on this very difficult matter.

Ignorance, and especially lack of knowledge of God, is always regarded as a bad thing in the New Testament. St Paul at Athens, addressing an audience with some philosophical pretensions, referred to the times of ignorance from which they had now to repent (Acts xvii.30). He told the Corinthians that it was a shameful thing to have no knowledge of God (1 Cor. xv.34), and he described Gentiles as "darkened in their understanding, alienated from the life of God because of the ignorance that is in them" (Eph. iv.18). St Peter too spoke

of the passions of the former ignorance of his readers (1 Pet. 1.14).
These are not examples of a Hellenistic intellectualism being
superimposed on the simplicity of the Gospel.   Our Lord
Himself had included "foolishness" or "lack of sense" among
the evil things which come from within and defile a man (Mk.
vii.22).   This is in agreement with Old Testament teaching;
Nabal, the fool in name as well as in nature, is on his wife's
testimony an ill-natured fellow (1 Sam. xxv.25).

Throughout the whole Old Testament, and particularly
in the Wisdom literature, a large place is given to knowledge.
Knowledge there is not the knowledge of abstract principles,
but the direct apprehension of reality—the kind of knowledge
we have of people we "know" as friends.   In particular to
know God is the chief duty of man (Dt. iv.39; Is. xliii.10;
Hos. vi.6), but such knowledge is our response to God's
knowing of man in such a way that He chooses individual
men and cares for them (Am. iii.2; Jer. 1.5).   The knowledge
of God is mediated through knowledge of the Law, but even
this is a knowledge involving man's whole being, emotion and
will as well as intellect (e.g. Ps. cxix.127 f.).

In this chapter we shall enquire into the knowledge that
is necessary for Christian goodness by considering two groups
of people—the one prominent in the Gospels, the other not
explicitly mentioned in the New Testament at all.   The
Pharisees lacked what is essential in religious knowledge,
although they would have been shocked at this accusation.
The Gnostics set too much value on a knowledge of the wrong
kind.   Both have their successors in the modern world, and we
may easily be misled by them.

§ 2

The Pharisees were people who prided themselves on their
religious knowledge as contrasted with that of the "crowd
who do not know the law" (Jn. vii.48, 49).   "The Pharisee,"
wrote Bonhoeffer, "is that extremely admirable man who
subordinates his entire life to his knowledge of good and evil. . . .
For the sake of avoiding any lapse his entire thought is
strenuously devoted night and day to the anticipation of the
whole immense range of possible conflicts, to the reaching of

a decision in these conflicts, and to the determination of his own choice."[1] Nor was their knowledge without results in action. Josephus speaks of the "great testimony . . . the cities bear them on account of their constant practice of virtue both in the actions of their lives and in their conversation."[2]

Both in the Gospels and in the Talmud there are, however, indications of defects in Pharisaic morality. Many of them practised virtue ostentatiously, to be seen and praised by men (Mt. VI.1-18); the Jerusalem Talmud refers to one kind of Pharisee as carrying his religious duties upon his shoulder for purposes of display.[3] Again their morality too often consisted in making rules for other people, putting burdens on others that they themselves did not attempt to carry (Mt. XXIII.1-4). Even worse, they showed a lack of sensitivity in discriminating between what was really important in their moral heritage and what was secondary and trivial; thus they tithed garden herbs (Mt. XXIII.23), and rejected the commandment of God in order to keep their own tradition (Mk. VII.9). The Jerusalem Talmud refers to the calculating Pharisee, who performs a good deed and then a bad deed, setting one off against the other.[4] The result was an inconsistency between their outward appearance and their inner nature; they became often without deliberate insincerity the whited sepulchres of our Lord's denunciation (Mt. XXIII.27).

Our Lord repeatedly called the Pharisees and their associates "hypocrites." The Aramaic word *hanifa*, which he probably used, indicated perversity, but may have developed nuances of meaning nearer to the Greek ὑποκριτής.[5] The Greek word commonly meant a play-actor, and we assume too readily that this word always signifies one who deliberately pretends to be what he is not or a dissembler. In the Gospels, where the word or its immediate cognates occurs twenty-four times, only in one story, told in the three Synoptic Gospels (Mk. XII.13-17; Mt. XXII.15-22; Lk. XX.20-6), is the emphasis necessarily on dissembling; the term is there applied to those

---

[1] Bonhoeffer, *Ethics*, p. 151.

[2] Flavius Josephus, *De antiquitatibus iudaicis*, XVIII. 1.3.

[3] *Jerusalem Talmud*, Berakoth, 14b.

[4] *Jerusalem Talmud*, Sotah, 22b.

[5] P. Joüon, "Ὑποκριτής dans l'Évangile et Hebreu 'hanef,'" in *Recherches de science religieuse*, XX (1930), pp. 312-16.

who pretended to ask Jesus an honest question about the propriety of paying taxes to Rome, but who were really trying to get Him into trouble. There were certainly such deliberate frauds among the Pharisees, as in most religious groups; but while the Talmud makes clear the ostentation and casuistry of many Pharisees, it does not suggest deliberate insincerity. People who traverse sea and land to make one proselyte (Mt. xxiii.15) are not usually insincere in their religious pretensions.

It appears, indeed, that the Pharisees themselves were quite unconscious of the hypocrisy with which our Lord chided them. The sayings in Mt. xxiii in which the Pharisees are called hypocrites are interrupted by others in which they are referred to as blind (vss. 16, 17, 26) "It is sad not to see any good in goodness,"[6] and the final condemnation of the Pharisees lies not in their insincerity but in their failure to recognise the perfect goodness that was Christ's. Anderson Scott, in elucidating the blindness of the Pharisees, compares it with what we may charitably call the blind spot in the moral perception of some outstanding Christians—Richard Baxter's attitude to witchcraft or George Whitefield's advocacy of slavery.[7] What is amply clear from the Gospels is that the blindness of the Pharisees was no isolated blind spot but a fundamental distortion of moral vision. This was not due to deliberate pretence; it was a more deep-seated malady. One result of it was certainly to make the Pharisees believe that they were better than they really were, but in this public opinion to some extent agreed with them.

The Pharisee was a play-actor or hypocrite, not chiefly in the modern sense of being a dissembler, but as "one whose doings in a play have no moral or religious significance in his case, whether he plays virtue or vice."[8] When John Gielgud plays Hamlet, his vacillating irresolution, however deeply felt by Gielgud at the moment, has nothing to do with Gielgud's own moral character. It was thus with the goodness of the Pharisees; they played their parts as religious men conscientiously, if a little ostentatiously as playboys are apt to do.

[6] N. V. Gogol, *Notebook for 1846*, quoted title-page of N. Berdyaev, *The Destiny of Man*, London 1937.

[7] C. Anderson Scott, *New Testament Ethics*, Cambridge 1930, pp. 45 f.

[8] D. Matheson, "Actors—Christ's Word of Scorn," in *Expository Times*, xli (1930), p. 333.

Their characteristic practices—almsgiving, prayer, fasting, the paying of tithes, the pursuing of proselytes, and the ceremonial ablutions—had lost much of their original religious meaning and relevance.

The Pharisees were obviously very religious people and yet they had missed the heart of true religion. They knew, and were right in knowing, that God demanded holiness of living, but they failed to realise that such goodness is always and only the gift of God's grace, and never the result of human effort—the outcome of the human knowledge of good and evil. The result was that they thought of their good deeds as the products of their own virtue and forgot that they owed everything to God. Oman expressed this by saying that the essence of hypocrisy is "to regard our privileges as merits."[9] When morality no longer has its source and power in the grace of God, it inevitably ceases to look on human need with the loving-kindness and justice of God. Ellul defines hypocrisy as "the giving up any attempt to live out one's religion in the world."[10] The Pharisees certainly attempted to live *their* religion, but it was no longer a religion that really knew God's grace, and, as a consequence, it no longer had any vital contact with human need. This is illustrated in one example that Matthew gives of the hypocrisy of the Pharisees—their ability to read the signs of the weather but their inability to read the signs of the times (Mt. xvi.3). (The question which follows in Luke's version and which is addressed to the multitudes and not the Pharisees; "And why do you not judge for yourselves what is right?" (Lk. xii.56) suggests that our Lord is at least including the moral signs of the times.) The Pharisees, while ready enough to give scientific forecasts of the weather—a pursuit in which their long practice in casuistical calculations might help them—were quite out of their depth when faced with real moral situations. They were blindly following man-made traditions even when faced with such an obvious moral need as the care of ageing parents (Mk. vii.13). It is an old error to suppose that the man whose mind is truly fixed on God will be withdrawn from all concern with the world. The very fact that the Christian learns to look on mankind with

[9] Oman, *Grace and Personality*, p. 179.
[10] Ellul, *Presence*, p. 14.

God's own love and concern means that he comes to see the really important moral issues—the signs of the times—in a way that the unbeliever cannot, and he does not waste his time on casuistical trifles. There is another consequence of the Pharisees' failure to know the grace of God. Once the inspiration of God's love and care for men does not have a part in morality, human approval becomes of paramount importance, and the Pharisee did his good works to be seen of men (Mt. vi.1, 2, 5).

"Morals without religion," is a slogan of our time, but the Pharisee stands as a warning that the mere pursuit of goodness for goodness' sake, however admirable an ideal it may appear, is fraught with the gravest moral danger. Nor is this danger confined to the humanist or the member of the ethical society which deliberately leaves out religion. The Pharisees were outstandingly religious people; their concern was with religious rather than specifically moral duties. A religious man can lose touch with God and his fellow men in his absorption with ecclesiastical rules and theological dilemmas almost as easily as the unbeliever, and his visible religious pretensions make his condition more despicable. Bonhoeffer in his treatment of the Pharisees[11] reminds us that the knowledge of good and evil was the bitter reward of man's first disobedience, and that such knowledge is indeed a curse, so long as it is divorced from the knowledge that is man's real good according to the teaching of Jesus—the knowledge of the will of the Heavenly Father. Censoriousness of others, an ostentatious display of piety, a casuistical emphasis on petty details, and the loss of a sense of what is vital in morality are the products of the human knowledge of good and evil, which is man's self-made substitute for obedience to the Word of God.

All this is very significant for the world of today, a world in which we too readily assume that we are no longer hypocrites like the unfortunate Pharisees whom our Lord denounced, or like our own immediate Victorian ancestors. Our knowledge of good and evil does not take the form of casuistical deductions or carefully weighed moral decisions; it takes rather the form of detailed planning for our future welfare, as if we knew all the answers. The failure of our planners to anticipate

[11] Bonhoeffer, *Ethics*, pp. 151-61.

such a comparatively simple economic fact as the fall in demand for coal should make us a little less confident in planning for traffic problems in the seventies or the world's population in the twenty-first century. It is, of course, the duty of statesmen to plan ahead, but it would be wiser planning if it were guided more by obedience to the revealed will of God than by human calculations. The commandments of God with their consideration for the weak and helpless can still be rejected in a determination to adhere to the traditions of men, although these traditions are now the economic laws of free enterprise rather than rules for the observances of piety. Again, is it not time that the Church bore a clear witness that the saving of young people, for whom we all profess such concern today, is not a matter of increased facilities for amusement or athletics or even education, useful as these things may be in an auxiliary way, but a matter of personal commitment to Christ? There is something fundamentally Pharisaic about our emphasis on good, healthy, Christian living, and our fear of heart-searching religious experience. The Pharisees separated themselves from the life of the world, and then failed to see the real purpose of God in their own religious institutions like the Sabbath. When the Church turns in on itself today, there is a similar danger of making a great bother over our own denominational catchwords, like "apostolic succession" or "the priesthood of all believers," without any attempt to see what these things really mean in the Word and purpose of God. That was the way of the Pharisees.

§ 3

The great Gnostic systems belong to a period later than that of the New Testament, but we find even there Christians at Corinth, who claimed to possess γνῶσις or knowledge (1 Cor. VIII.1), a heresy with marked Gnostic tendencies at Colossae (Col. II.8-23), and Christians at Ephesus who needed to be assured that Jesus came in the flesh (II Jn. 7) and not as an immaterial manifestation, which was the view of certain Gnostics. The tendencies which gave rise to Gnosticism were certainly at work in New Testament times, and included a tendency to syncretism or the combining of elements from different religions, the tendency to assimilate Christian teaching to the thought and language of educated men in the Hellenistic world, and,—what chiefly concerns us here—the tendency to believe that salvation depends primarily on knowledge. This last tendency had, as we have already suggested, a long Greek tradition behind it, and it was natural and expedient that, when Christian missionaries presented their Gospel to the Hellenistic world, they should, as far as they honestly could, use the language of Greek culture and try to fit their message into the accepted world-view. This was easier to do with regard to knowledge because it is likely that our Lord Himself and the first Christian preachers had emphasised a saving knowledge. "This is eternal life that they know thee the only true God, and Jesus Christ whom thou hast sent" (Jn. XVII.3), is the witness to a Christian gnosis in John. Similarly St Paul seeks for his Ephesian readers "a spirit of wisdom and of revelation in the knowledge of him, having the eyes of your hearts enlightened" (Eph. 1.17-18).

In developed Gnosticism man's evil condition was held to be the result of his fall from the sphere of pure spirit down into the world of matter, in which he is now imprisoned. The way of moral and spiritual restoration is through an intellectual understanding of our human nature, and particularly of the influences by which it became corrupted in the course of its descent from the "fullness" of God's presence through the various planetary spheres to the earth-bound life. Christian Gnostics held that the mission of Jesus was to provide such intellectual knowledge, and that men, by the very act of receiving it, gain moral emancipation. The Gnostics were anticipating a characteristic view of our own scientific age that the understanding of the causes of a morbid condition either in an individual or in a society is not only a preliminary step towards a cure, as all would admit, but has a curative effect in itself. This is seen most clearly in the practice of psycho-analysis. It has its measure of truth, which determined the Greek maxim "Know thyself," and St Paul put it into Christian practice in Rom. VII. Yet an intellectual comprehension of the causes of our moral corruption, whether obtained by Gnostic cosmologies or by Freudian psychology, is not the heart of the Christian Gospel, as the Gnostics supposed. Scientific knowledge is not saving knowledge, although the wise Christian will not despise any help that science, and particularly psychology, can give.

The Gnostic who claims to understand the roots of moral evil may easily fall into one or other of two dangers. He may think that the man who knows is above the conventional distinction between right and wrong and so he becomes an antinomian, like the Nicolaitans mentioned in the New Testament (Rev. II.6, 15) and other Gnostic groups. The modern psychologist, having traced the moral law to its sources in primitive taboos and repressions, may take the quite unscientific step of supposing that the moral law has therefore no authority at the present time. He may be too wise to take such a view himself but this is certainly the effect of his teaching on many young people today. (It is well to remember that the Christian theologian's disparagement of Christian ethics may have a similar effect.) The other danger is a false asceticism. The Gnostic, who attributed man's evil to the influence of matter, including his own body, practised ascetic techniques in order to rid the soul of such material influences. Modern man still falsely regards his material environment as the sole cause of many of his physical and moral ills, but he meets this not by asceticism but by an exaggerated faith in improved material conditions and improved medical techniques, as if good houses, good schools, and well-balanced diets would save men from sin. There is a subsidiary place both for ascetic practices and for improved material conditions in advancing the moral life, and there are still Christian groups who emphasise, or overemphasise, both of them, but such things are at the circumference of Christian morality. They certainly do not constitute the knowledge in which John finds the secret of eternal life.

One of the writings found in a Gnostic library at Nag Hammadi in Egypt in 1945 is entitled the Gospel of Truth and may be the work written by the Gnostic Valentinus about A.D. 145, perhaps just before he left the Catholic Church. It is not, like the New Testament Gospels, an account of the life and teachings of Jesus; it is a gospel in the sense in which St Paul refers to his own message (most fully expressed in Romans) as "my gospel." While St Paul preaches a gospel of salvation

through God's act of justification in Jesus Christ, the Gospel
of Truth preaches a gospel of salvation through the knowledge
of God given in the teaching of Christ.[12] What that knowledge
is does not appear very clearly in the text of the Gospel of
Truth; it is certainly a more metaphysical knowledge than
that given in the New Testament, although there are hints of
evangelical themes in the spirit of the later Pauline and Johannine epistles. Moral perfection is the goal of this gospel, for
the concluding lines say; "His children are perfect and worthy
of His Name, for they are children, such as He the Father
loves."[13] There are none, however, of the practical moral
teachings that we find in the concluding chapters of some of
St Paul's letters or of the explicit injunctions to love the
brethren that we find in the Johannine writings. The Gnostics
appear to have found in a philosophical "knowledge of the
Father" a deep intellectual satisfaction. Theologians still find
such satisfaction in constructing a coherent philosophical
system, and to do so is one of the lofty aspirations of our human
nature. The higher mathematicians have a somewhat similar
aspiration, but they have commonly realised that their higher
intellectual flights have little relevance to the checking of
bills or the measuring of floor areas. Theologians have not
always understood so clearly what they are doing and have
imagined that by their theological speculations they are helping
men to live the Christian life.

§ 4

What then is the Christian knowledge that leads to goodness?
Here again we answer in the light of the Old Testament
conception of knowledge. There is no separate department
of Christian knowledge exclusively concerned with moral
practice; the nearest things to that are our knowledge of our
Lord's example and of the distinctively ethical teachings of
parts of the New Testament. What we believe from faith and
experience is that the knowledge of the whole Gospel does

---

[12] A thesis developed by L. Cerfaux, "De Saint Paul à 'l'Évangile de la Vérité'," in *New Testament Studies*, v (1959), pp. 103-12.

[13] *Evangelium Veritatis*, edd. M. Malinine, H. C. Puech and G. Quispel, Zürich 1956, f.xxii, r, lines 20-4.

have a real power to make men good. It is, to begin with, a knowledge of historical facts, particularly the facts of what God did in Jesus Christ. Such facts differ from the propositions of Gnostic philosophy in that they can be grasped by all, even by little children. The truths discovered by Gnosticism or philosophical theology or mystical experience may be helpful to people of particular temperaments, but they are not truths essential for the Christian faith that leads to goodness. It is not only, however, a knowledge of facts, but a personal knowledge of God the Father, as revealed in His giving of Himself to us in Jesus Christ. It is not only the knowledge of God given in the teachings of Jesus, which the Gnostics emphasised, but the direct knowing of a person. This is the knowledge which belongs to little children, as both the canonical Gospels (Mt. xi.25; Lk. x.21) and the Gospel of Truth[14] realise. Little children cannot understand the intricacies of either Gnostic or modern theology, but they can know people, and so they can know Jesus Christ and the Father through Him. Incidentally the person known through a book can be a very real person to a child, and a child may be at an advantage here in reading the Gospel story. This knowledge takes possession of a man's whole being, of his feeling and will as well as his intellect. Educationists know that the knowledge that matters is neither the possession of facts which are valuable chiefly for "Top of the Form" contests nor the acquisition of skills for immediate practical use. The knowledge that matters is that which captures the child's imagination so that he lives with it. It is here in religion that love and knowledge meet, and this is the knowledge that does lead, however long the road may be, to real goodness.

Literature

D. MATHESON, " 'Actors'—Christ's word of scorn," in *Expository Times*, XLI (1930), p. 333 f.

C. ANDERSON SCOTT, *New Testament Ethics*, Cambridge 1930, pp. 40-7.

D. BONHOEFFER, *Ethics*, London 1955, pp. 151-61. Translation of *Ethik*, Munich 1949.

[14] *Evangelium Veritatis*, edd. M. Malinine, H. C. Puech and G. Quispel, f.x, r, lines 28-30.

L. H. Marshall, *The Challenge of New Testament Ethics*, London 1948, pp. 60-2.

P. Joüon, " Ὑποκριτής dans l'Évangile et Hebreu 'hanef'" in *Recherch esde science religieuse*, xx (1930), pp. 312-16.

Evangelium Veritatis, edd. M. Malinine, H. C. Puech, and G. Quispel, Zürich 1956.

R. M. Wilson, *The Gnostic Problem*, London 1958.

L. Cerfaux, "De Saint Paul à'l Évangile de la Vérité'," in *New Testament studies*, v (1959), pp. 103-112.

Chapter VII

The New Testament Attitude
to Law and Justice

THE word "justice" does not occur in the English authorised
version of the New Testament, although in some modern
translations it here and there replaces the more frequent
"judgment." "Judgment" is not merely an archaic usage;
it does indicate that the Bible speaks more of particular just
acts and decisions than of the abstract quality of justice. The
Old Testament contained a record of God's judgments in the
past, and these, as we have already seen,[1] included acts of
vindication and deliverance as well as sentences of doom. It is
in these judgments of God that we lay hold of the justice of
God.[2] The Bible gives us no comprehensive theory of that
justice any more than it gives us a systematic law code; we
learn of God's justice from vivid examples in the course of
His varied dealings with His people. It was part of the New
Testament faith that, as John puts it, "the Father . . . has given
all judgment to the Son (Jn. v.22), and "has given him authority
to execute judgment because he is the Son of man (Jn. v.27).
While Christ's judgment includes the judgment of condemnation it is primarily a judgment of deliverance: "For God sent
His Son into the world not to condemn the world but that the
world might be saved through him" (Jn. III.17). Jesus sees
that His judgment is just not in any abstract standard of equity
but in the fact that He is doing His Father's will (Jn. v.30).
For St Paul too, the final judgment is now the judgment-seat
of Christ (II Cor. v.10).

We need not doubt that there lay behind the Biblical idea
of judgment that common notion of justice which is found,

[1] See p. 4 f.
[2] Ellul, *Theological Foundation*, p. 46: "Only in judgment do we grasp Justice."

69

however vaguely, in all men—"the rendering to each man his
due" of Natural Law. The judge of all the earth necessarily
does what men at their best regard as right.[3]   Such justice is
commonly held to demand the ignoring of all personal considerations, for in human judges a regard for persons leads to
partiality. The justice of God is, however, saturated with an
interest in persons which takes into account the particular
characteristics and needs of each individual. That justice of
this kind can be consistent with impartiality is demonstrated
by the practice of juvenile courts at their best. Equity,
including fair retribution, has its place in the decisions of these
courts, but the dominant consideration for the good magistrate
is the welfare of the young person concerned—obviously a
matter of personal interest. The long Lutheran tradition
which makes the justice of the Gospel the antithesis of all
worldly justice is here inadequate; the magistrate is practising
the justice of the Gospel within limits imposed by his office.
The father in the story of the Prodigal Son was not less just
than the elder brother. The latter had the ordinary human
view of justice; his erring brother did not deserve the fatted
calf and the rest, and it was not fair that he should enjoy them.
The father, acknowledging that all his worldly estate belonged
to the elder son (for Gospel justice never excludes equity), saw
a larger justice. Whatever be the cost to the family God's
justice demands the restoration of the lost son; one does not
demand a cash settlement of accounts in the name of justice
from a man who has been dead and is alive again. Even when
God condemns and punishes, his interest is still personal; "the
Lord disciplines him whom he loves" (Heb. xii.6). For this
reason C. H. Dodd's interpretation of the wrath of God as
"an inevitable process of cause and effect in a moral universe"[4]
is inadequate; the reaction of God to evil is fundamentally a
personal reaction, although it has nothing of the arbitrary
capriciousness of our human anger.

[3] Gen. xviii.25, which is neater and more expressive in Hebrew, "Shall not
the *shophet* do *mishpat?*"
[4] C. H. Dodd, *The Epistle of Paul to the Romans*, Moffatt New Testament Commentaries, London 1932, p. 23.

§ 2

All New Testament writers, in so far as they suggest a theory of law at all, regard it as the command of God. This was in their view directly and historically true of the Law of Moses, but it was also true of the law written on men's hearts (Rom. II.15) and even of the law of the Roman authorities who were "instituted by God" (Rom. XIII.1). It is true also of the new law proclaimed in the Sermon on the Mount; Jesus' tone is not, like that of the Rabbis, "academic, but final, prophetic" —the word of "supreme authority."[5] What Jesus and St Paul said about right conduct is not mere pious exhortation; it is *law*, and the requirement of law as such is that it cannot be violated with impunity. This may explain the emphasis in the New Testament on rewards in heaven and punishments in unquenchable fire, which many find repugnant to a gospel of grace. Without these sanctions, pictured in the apocalyptic imagery of the time, the law of Christ might sound like the moral platitudes preached by Stoic teachers. Men still too commonly regard them as such.

Our Lord knew as certainly as St Paul and the modern critic that there had been incorporated into the God-given Law of Moses (and presumably also into other codes), very human elements, "making void the word of God through your tradition" (Mk. VII.13); such additions did not have that personal concern so clearly implied in the two chief commandments of love to God and love to neighbour. The fact that even Jewish rabbis regarded some precepts of the law as more important than others indicates that the written law was not to be applied mechanically. If a law, like the law of the Sabbath or the law forbidding laymen to eat the shewbread or even the law condemning an adulteress to be stoned, were in a particular case to violate the great realities of God's mercy and steadfast love (revealed in the law as a whole), then our Lord had no hesitation in disobeying that particular law. Personal consideration must come before abstract principle.

Yet our Lord made a clear statement with regard to the permanent validity of the Law of Moses; "Think not that I

---

[5] D. Daube, *The New Testament and Rabbinic Judaism*, henceforth cited as *N.T. and Rabbinic Judaism*, London 1956, p. 58.

F

have come to abolish the law and the prophets; I have come
not to abolish them but to fulfil them. For truly, I say to you,
till heaven and earth pass away, not an iota, not a dot, will
pass from the law until all is accomplished . . . For I tell you,
unless your righteousness exceeds that of the scribes and
Pharisees, you will never enter the kingdom of heaven" (Mt.
v.17-20). Some comments must be made on this. (*a*) The Law
includes not only particular regulations with their appropriate
sanctions; it includes the whole Old Testament revelation—
prophets as well as law—with its emphasis on God's mercy
and faithfulness, which demand the love and loyalty of His
own people. (*b*) Christians are called to be saints, and the
outcome of the Gospel of grace should be the production of
better men than the scribes and Pharisees, men who are more
forgiving and more pure (to take two of the illustrations given
in the latter part of Matthew v). The Christian way of
attainment is certainly not that of Pharisaic legalism, but its
goal is farther along the same road. (*c*) These teachings are
warnings against antinomianism, which is the devil's mis-
interpretation of God's grace, uttered with the vivid hyperbole
of an Eastern teacher. Taken literally, Mt. v.18 certainly
contradicts the fundamental teaching of Jesus, which cares
everything for the spirit of God's law and nothing for the iotas
and dots of this verse. T. W. Manson believed that this
saying in its original form was "bitter irony,"[6] and A. M.
Hunter considers that the words as they stand in their present
context can hardly be the words of Jesus.[7] Jesus Himself
relaxed the Sabbath law, annulled Moses' provisions for
divorce, and rejected the rules about ritual defilement. What
Jesus is doing here is proclaiming the paramount importance
of the moral law in the shock-producing way which a twentieth-
century professor, nurtured in the philosophy of language, is
unlikely to use, but which an Eastern teacher uses naturally
as a method of instruction.

When St Paul uses the word "law," he has almost always
at the back of his mind the Torah, which was the law that he
knew best. In many passages he is referring explicitly to this
Law of Moses and calls it "*the* law" (Rom. viii.3, 4; Gal. iv.21,

---

[6] T. W. Manson, *The Sayings of Jesus*, London 1949, p. 135.
[7] A. M. Hunter, *Design for Life*, London 1953, p. 43.

etc.); but there are also passages in which he is still writing about the Torah, in which he does not use the definite article (Rom. v.20, x.4; Gal. ii.19, etc.); in these he is probably thinking of the Torah in its quality of being law rather than in the aspect of its being the special code of the Jewish people. St Paul, like Philo and others, undoubtedly regards the Law of Moses, given by God the Creator, as the supreme expression of what we call natural law (Rom. ii.14, 20), but other codes, like that of the Roman authorities (Rom. xiii.1, 4), are also expressions in a lesser degree of natural God-given law, and St Paul certainly includes these in the many passages when he refers to law generally without the definite article (Rom. ii.12, 14, iii.20 f., iv.15, etc.). Even when St Paul uses the word "law" most widely and ambiguously (as he does) there always remain overtones derived from its use as meaning Torah. The one exception to this is where St Paul uses "law" for a principle of evil (Rom. vii.23, viii.2), but the word still retains the imperative connotation it has elsewhere.

In spite of all that St Paul had to say about Christians being no longer "under the law" (e.g. Rom. vi.14; Gal. iii.24, 25, v.18), he too knew that so long as Christ's followers are ambiguously placed as citizens of heaven in a world very much under the sway of the old order, there must be some kind of law. He was not greatly interested either in Jewish law, which he saw to be outdated, or in Roman law, which Christians had to accept as part of the world in which they lived; and for him the Gospel was far more relevant to human need than any law. In all probability he could not foresee a time when Christian principles might find expression even in the positive laws of a state. It is not surprising that in the New Testament we have only hints of the place of law in a Christian community, but some things are clear.

1. Without some law and order, life in a community of imperfect Christians and vast numbers of unbelievers is not possible, and this was probably one reason why St Paul enjoined obedience to the Roman authorities; it was clearly Roman law and not the Law of Moses that was now keeping tendencies to lawlessness in restraint. Brunner says that "we need this rude order [of law and custom] as a framework for all the more

refined and spiritual forms of life which are obedient to God."[7]
We must beware of talking depreciatingly of secular justice as
if it were "rude" and unworthy of Christian consideration.
Lord Keynes described how the breakdown of such secular
justice at the Treaty of Versailles affected a strict Jew, Dr
Melchior. "The breach of promise, the breach of discipline,
the decay of honourable behaviour, the betrayal of under-
takings by the one party and the insincere acceptance by
the other of impossible conditions which it was not intended
to carry out, . . . it was these offences against The Word which
so much wounded him. . . . The Tablets of the Law . . . had
perished meanly."[8]   In a country with a Christian *ethos*,
however nebulous, justice may be the normal "expression of
love in impersonal relations."[9]   Our love for the neighbour
whom we do not meet on the Jericho road or elsewhere reaches
its most practical and comprehensive expression in the provisions made for that neighbour's needs by the Welfare State.
The law of the land is not merely a negative barrier against
the forces of disorder; it can be a positive expression of Christian
concern, and it is the business of Christians to try to make it
this.

2. Law elicits a knowledge of wrong-doing, and so in-
directly a realisation of our own sinfulness and helplessness in
the face of evil. St Paul says; "If it had not been for the law,
I should not have known sin" (Rom. vii.7), and goes on to
give his classical account of the divided human heart apart
from Christ. Such a knowledge has often led men to Christ,
although it is wrong to limit Christian experience to this
single pattern, for, as Brunner reminds us, it is God Himself,
and not the law, who is ultimately the schoolmaster leading us
to Christ,[10] and He is not limited to one method.   It is often
forgotten today that the law of a country too has, as one of its
functions, the education of the citizen, and especially of the
young citizen, in the knowledge of what is wrong.   One of the
dangers of our present-day multiplication of government
regulations is that the simple-minded youth, seeing the

[7] Brunner, *Divine Imperative*, p. 141.
[8] J. M. Keynes, *Two Memoirs*, London 1949, p. 70 f.
[9] Micklem, *Law and the Laws*, p. 10.
[10] Brunner, *Divine Imperative*, p. 146 f.

innocuousness of disobeying many of these regulations, makes the naive inference that all laws are equally made to be broken. This is a consideration which must be taken into account when changes in the law, such as the abolition of capital punishment or the removal of homosexual acts from the category of crimes, are proposed. Does the proposed change in law mean that people, because of this change, will no longer regard murder or homosexual practices as the evil things they really are? Such a possibility must be taken into account.

3. Even for the committed Christian, fully conscious of his Christian liberty, law may still provide useful guidance as to the best use of his freedom. We can still learn a good deal about the Christian style of life from the Law of Moses, if that law is studied imaginatively in the spirit of Christ. Are we as concerned practically about the dangers of children on the roads as the Deuteronomic law was about the dangers of children on the flat roofs of houses without protecting parapets? (Dt. xxii.8). Even such a detailed work of casuistry (in the best sense) as the Highway Code is, for the Christian, not merely a means of avoiding the attentions of the police, but a guide to Christian courtesy on the roads—a most practical and necessary application of Christian love today.

§ 3

In spite of all that St Paul says about the law being spiritual, holy, and good (Rom. vii.12, 14), there are the seeds of abuse, corruption, and even injustice in every legal code, and St Paul knew it well. This had proved to be the case even with the God-given Law of Moses, when it fell into priestly and Pharisaic hands, and it can still be true of the rules of a boys' club or of the laws of a state, as well as of an ecclesiastical system of casuistry. The New Testament is fully alive to these dangers.

1. It is desirable that there should be rules to show us what is right, as in the Highway Code, but the legislator, in his determination to avoid that vagueness which invalidates positive law, tends to make constant additions to it. So rules tend to increase in number and detail until a multitude of innocent activities become transgressions of the law. In the heyday of government regulations at the end of World War II, a timber

merchant said that it was impossible to know and, still more, to carry out all the regulations about his own particular business. This was very probably the case with the Jewish law in New Testament times, as it certainly was by the time of the Talmud. When St Paul speaks of the law "coming in to increase the trespass" (Rom. v.20), and says that "where there is no law there is no transgression" (Rom. iv.15), this proliferation of detailed rules may be part of what he has in mind. The moral for the modern maker of laws is to keep the laws as few and simple as the complexities of the modern world permit.

2. St Paul speaks of sinful passions being aroused by the law itself (Rom. vii.5). There is in most men the urge to enter a path where there is a notice saying "Trespassers will be prosecuted," and this urge, we may hope, explains in part the bootlegging during the days of American prohibition or the incursions made into the black market in times of rationing by otherwise respectable people. "Gainsay, and the blood's on fire," is Mary Webb's account of it in *Precious Bane*. St Paul, however, may be pointing to something far more sinister. When legalism holds sway, a demonic element may come into the process of law itself. Two of its most horrid manifestations are a sadistic pleasure taken in punishing the guilty, as by hanging judges like the notorious Judge Jeffreys or even by certain schoolmasters, and the fascination that the eagerly-sought details of the most unsavoury crimes seem to have had for some ecclesiastical courts in the past. There can be little doubt that in such cases the legal condemnation of evil is concealing a deeper stimulation of the evil inclinations of men's hearts.

3. Codified law tends to be static and not easily adaptable to new conditions. St Paul contrasts the bondage of the "old written code" to the freedom of the Spirit (Rom. vii.6). This bondage is seen in certain groups today, who appear to oppose on principle any changes in laws, however antiquated. Christians should realise the limitations and dangers of pro- hibitive laws, and should be working positively for new and more imaginative legislation in the spirit of Christian freedom on such vexed matters as Sunday observance, gambling, and the sale of alcoholic liquors.

4. People who limit their religious duty to the carrying out of certain external rules are tempted to feel, like some of the Pharisees, that they are justified by the works of the law (Gal. II.16). This tendency still exists in such odd forms as one man being satisfied that all is well because he has made his communions, or another maintaining that he is just as good as his neighbour in matters of conduct, and this proves him a good Christian.

5. St Paul found that there was a danger that obedience to the law might become a kind of slavery (Rom. VI.16; Gal. IV.21-V.1). A man can feel burdened and oppressed with the demands of the law, just as he feels oppressed with a sense of guilt. Positive law is inevitably characterised by some force of restriction or coercion, but the less conscious citizens are of this the better. In our own country, many people do not feel the law oppressive; they have never been inside a lawcourt, and the policeman is their protector and friend. This has not been the experience of some other countries, even in our own time, where respectable people have lived in constant fear of the law and its minions. The Torah, which had been a source of joy to Jews in the past, had, through an increasing legalism, become to St Paul a tyranny.

6. "By works of the law shall no one be justified" (Gal. II.16, III.11; Rom. III.20). The Jewish law had no power to deliver men from evil and make them acceptable to God. A modern example may illustrate its failure. The American prohibition law of 1920 was a law with a saving purpose; its primary aim was not to punish alcoholics but to save the citizens of the United States from the evils of intemperance. But this law did not work and had to be repealed; it was, as most social reformers agree, the wrong way to deal with intemperance. St Paul saw in a similar fashion that the holy and just Law of Moses did not work. The Pharisees would have denied this because they had lost the Old Testament idea of God's justice comprehending deliverance and salvation. So long as the Law was used to separate Pharisees from the people of the land, or Jews from sinners of the Gentiles, it was a most useful instrument of discrimination; but when it comes to justifying a fallen world, the Law of Moses and every other code of laws prove useless. St Paul, however, retained the

word "justify," and this indicates that law and justice still have a place in the Christian evangel. The Christian aim of justice is still the restoration of the offender. Many dislike this view, because they confuse it with the sentimentality that would do away with the sterner sanctions of the law. The Bible has none of that sentimentality; both Proverbs and Hebrews take physical punishment for granted. The reason for such severity, however, is the justification or, as our modern jargon would put it, the rehabilitation of one whom the Lord loves.

In view of all these weaknesses, which are inherent in every legal code, Christians will always regard critically the laws of the society to which they belong, and will realise their interim and provisional character. They cannot but remember that the processes of the Jewish religious law and of the Roman secular law together led to the unjust crucifixion of their Lord. Yet, after His example, they will submit to the punishments of those laws.

§ 4

St Paul twice refers to the "law of Christ" (Gal. vi.2; 1 Cor. ix.19-23), and so suggests that the moral precepts of the New Testament have still some of the characteristics of law. He certainly does not mean that our Lord laid down a systematic code of laws, which would have soon become dated and would have been subject to all our human relativities; every attempt to make detailed rules out of the teaching of the Gospel is a failure. What Jesus actually did was to provide vivid, occasional glimpses of what the law of Christ demands, in such a para-doxical way that not even the most literally minded can make rules out of them. He pictures, for example, the man stripping off his shirt and handing it to the Shylock who has seized his outer cloak as pledge, or the man having the trumpets blow a fanfare before he announces his latest public benefaction. Such a law "cannot really be broken up into specific injunctions, for its implications are developed anew in every fresh human situation."[11]   In these circumstances the most adequate formulation of this law might appear to be St Augustine's; "Love and do what you like."[12]   The New Testament is too

---

[11] H. Butterfield, *History and Human Relations*, London 1951, p. 42.
[12] Augustine, *In. Epist. Ioannis Tract.*, vii.8: "Dilige et quod vis fac."

realistic to leave it at that, for even Christian men do not love God as they should and are in any case too ignorant to know how this love shows itself in living. So we need our Lord's commands and St Paul's counsels. This is no ordinary law in this other respect, that it deals with the inner workings of the heart, such as the lustful look and the gust of anger. The Law of Moses had indeed taken one step in this direction in the tenth commandment, for it is clear that covetousness cannot be dealt with by the law courts like theft or murder. Again the range of application of Christ's law extends far beyond even the resident alien for whom the Mosaic code so humanely provided. The point of the parable of the good Samaritan is that the man whom we naturally regard as our enemy, be he Samaritan or Communist, proves himself to be the neighbour, whom the Law of Holiness enjoins us to love as we love ourselves.

St Paul presented Christian liberty in contrast to the Jewish law; "For freedom Christ has set us free" (Gal. v.1). So the interpretation we give of the law of Christ must not be inconsistent with Christian freedom. The man who is un-principled, with no order in his life, is not really free; he is the slave of every passing impulse. The Christian, by freely choosing to order his life according to the law of Christ, finds in His service perfect freedom. (There had been a time when a psalmist found something like that in the Law of Moses.) There is, however, a creative freedom in Christ's law. "It is a law capable of commanding men to do something which nobody has ever been instructed to do before, something perhaps which nobody has ever hitherto thought of. That is to say, it is a principle calculated to carry a human being to unpredictable readjustments of conduct or of attitude; and in the lives of the saints, it can be seen to have operated more like an instruction to adventure and originality, even carrying the surprises to the point of eccentricity."[13] Freedom is often interpreted today as the freedom to exploit one's fellow men, but such an interpretation is contrary both to the justice of Natural Law and the Biblical justice that implies deliverance.

How are the positive laws of a state related to this law of Christ? Lutherans have commonly held that the law of Christ

[13] Butterfield, *History and Human Relations*, p. 42.

belongs to the personal world of faith and not to the institutional world of justice. It is true that the New Testament does not explicitly raise this issue, for the early Christians were in no position to make or modify the laws of the Roman *imperium*, and this is the position in which many Christians still find themselves. Yet it seems likely that the laws of countries with long Christian traditions do have in part Christian presuppositions. The writ of *habeas corpus* does, for example, presuppose that man has the value of a child of God, and "where systems of law have arisen, as in . . . Russia, which implicitly deny that he is a child of God, there is no *habeas corpus*, and those who are displeasing to the authorities simply disappear leaving no trace."[14] Of course there can be no direct insertions into positive law of rules from the Sermon on the Mount or any other part of the New Testament. The laws of a state, in order to be effective, must be laws which many do observe and the rest can normally be expected to observe in view of the sanctions provided. We have already suggested that justice may be a natural expression of Christian love in impersonal relations, and it is reasonable that Christians should seek for laws which embody not only generally accepted notions of equity, but that distinctively Biblical justice which seeks deliverance from oppression and evil. After all, it is commonly accepted that the law of the land, like the justice of Yahweh, should protect its citizens from external oppression and physical injuries. Christians may well demand that the law should also protect men from temptations to evil. Of course an undue interference with that personal freedom which itself is part of our Christian heritage must be guarded against. What we here maintain is that deliverance from temptation is one factor to be taken into account, along with individual liberty and the maintenance of public order, in the determining of our laws about such things as gambling, prostitution, the sale of alcoholic liquors, and the control of entertainment. The state, too, according to St Paul, plays a part in the wrath of God, in which St Paul saw a natural, if personal, retribution of evil (Rom. xiii.1-5). Magistrates should be a terror to evildoers, not benevolent gentlemen over-conscious of the danger of themselves committing the same offences as those before

---

[14] Micklem, *Law and the Laws*, p. 18.

them. Yet at the same time a "Christian" country's legislation and judicial administration should play some positive part in answering the last petition of the Lord's Prayer; "Lead us not into temptation, but deliver us from evil."

Literature

C. H. DODD, *Gospel and Law*, Cambridge 1951.

E. BRUNNER, *The Divine Imperative*, London 1937, ch. XIV.

N. MICKLEM, *Law and the Laws*, Edinburgh 1952.

E. BRUNNER, *Justice and the Social Order*, London 1946, esp. pp. 102-8.

W. LILLIE, *The Law of Christ*, London 1956, chs. I and II.

H. KELSEN, "Justice in the Holy Scriptures," in *What is Justice?* Berkeley (California) 1957, pp. 25-81.

H. H. SCHREY, H. H. WALZ, and W. A. WHITEHOUSE, *The Biblical Doctrine of Justice and Law*, Ecumenical Biblical Studies VOL. III, London 1955.

Chapter VIII

The New Testament Attitude to the State

Two very different pictures of the state[1] can be found in
the Bible. The first, which in the Old Testament had
always Israel in mind, was the vision of a future kingdom
of great material wealth in which Israel would rule over all
other nations, but also a kingdom where God's law would be
so established that God would be truly its king. Consequently
some held that God's priests, as His representatives, would
have supreme power in the state. The idea that "the Lord
God was your king" went back at least as far as one version of
Saul's appointment to the throne (1 Sam. XII.12), and in this
view the earthly king held office only so long as he obeyed the
Heavenly King, of whom Samuel was at that time the mouth-
piece. In the early days of the Maccabees many Jews must
have hoped that this theocracy was at last beginning, but the
policies and characters of the later Hashmonean kings must
have brought sad disillusionment. In the literature of this
period we find two views of the coming kingdom; the one is of
a kingdom, spiritual, supernatural, and not of this world; the
other is of the traditional this-worldly kingdom, although some
felt that it too must come down from God out of heaven by a
special act of Divine intervention.

At the time of our Lord the Zealots were the party with a
definite programme for establishing the Kingdom of God by
the political and military means with which new earthly
kingdoms are commonly set up. The Zealots, whom Josephus
first mentions in connexion with the revolt of Judas of Gamala
at the beginning of the first century of our era, are not to be
regarded as mere anarchists, although their programme would
attract to their party brigands like Barabbas. Josephus calls

[1] These two approaches are suggested by R. Niebuhr, *The Nature and Destiny of
Man*, London 1943, VOL. II, ch. 9, §5. (p. 279).

two of their later leaders "sophists," the common Hellenistic term for teachers, and while we may hesitate to accept Cecil Roth's view that the sect of the Dead Sea Scrolls was a Zealot group, he certainly gives us reasons to think that the Zealots had a body of doctrine and a constructive programme of revolutionary reform.[2] Cullman argues convincingly that, in the eyes of the more honest of his enemies and particularly of the Romans, Jesus was a Zealot.[3] In Acts both the Jewish Gamaliel (Acts v.36-7) and the Roman tribune Claudius Lysias (Acts xxi.38), seem to regard the Christian movement as akin to the Zealot revolts. One of Jesus' own disciples, Simon, was a Zealot, who may have thought that he was following a new and more promising Zealot leader when he gave his loyalty to Jesus. (Cullmann suggests more fancifully that Judas Iscariot, Peter, and the two "sons of thunder" James and John, may also originally have been Zealots.)[4] The accusation made against Jesus that "we found this man perverting our nation, and forbidding us to give tribute to Caesar, and saying that he himself is Christ a king" (Lk. xxiii.2), was just the accusation that informers would make against a Zealot, and although Pilate knew in his heart that Jesus was no Zealot, the *titulus* on the Cross showed that Jesus was condemned for the characteristically Zealot crime of claiming to be "King of the Jews."

Jesus Himself, however, consistently refused to identify His kingdom with a political state. His temptations suggest that He may have been attracted by the Zealot dream of a free Jewish theocracy, for these were largely temptations to use the common means of the politician—economic advantages, showmanship, and sheer force—in establishing the promised kingdom. This temptation may have come again in Gethsemane; Jesus must have remembered the enthusiasm of the crowd on Palm Sunday and the poor resistance to His clearing of the court of the Gentiles in the Temple; some of His disciples were armed, and He knew that His Father would support Him with twelve legions of angels if He asked for them (Mt. xxvi.53). Jesus knew, as

---

[2] C. Roth, *The Historical Background of the Dead Sea Scrolls*, Oxford 1958.
[3] O. Cullmann, *The State in the New Testament*, henceforth cited as *State in N.T*, London 1957, ch. II.
[4] *Op. cit.*, pp. 15 ff.

He told Pilate at His trial, that His kingdom was not of this world, and could not be achieved by fighting in the fashion of worldly revolutions (Jn. XVIII.33-8). His kingship had to do with bearing witness to the truth, and this is still the relation of Christ's kingdom to earthly kingdoms. The function of the Christian Church facing the rulers of this world is to proclaim the truth, primarily the good news of salvation, but also the true condemnation of what is wrong, whether it be the adultery of a Herodias or the *apartheid* policy of the government of South Africa.

The idea of the Kingdom of God as an earthly kingdom did not disappear with the Zealots, nor is it confined to Jewish Zionists today. The teaching of St Paul (Gal. VI.16, Rom. X-XI) and others that the Church was the true Israel made it possible, once the Church had attained wealth and power, to think of it as an earthly kingdom. The Roman Church, in particular, retains so many of the forms and institutions of an ordinary kingdom that there can be little doubt that it has regarded one side of its mission very much in the way that some Jews, both prophets and Zealots, regarded the mission of the old Israel. Protestants have more often regarded the state as separate from, or even completely independent of, the Church, although they may hold that its rulers should be so conditioned by the teachings of the Church as to make it a powerful instrument for the establishment of Christ's coming kingdom. Faith in the social Gospel, in the United Nations, and in the virtue of the "good neighbour" state indicates a tendency in our own day to revive the old confusion between the Kingdom of God and political organisation. The truth underlying this confusion is one which the New Testament largely ignores because of the political circumstances of the early Church. The state is a God-given institution to meet the human need for community in the widest sense of that word. It had met this need in ancient Israel, but it no longer did so for conquered Jews under the Roman yoke. Jews in captivity had found a deeper fellowship in the synagogue, and Christians now found it in the Church. In the modern world both state and Church claim to meet that need, admittedly on different levels. In a new housing area the civic community centre and the Church with its halls and youth organisations seem to the outsider to be meeting the same community needs. There are those who tell us that Christians can best express their faith by giving whole-hearted service in the centres organised by the state, and, unless the Church can give a deeper and more personal fellowship than the better-provided state centres can give, there seems little reason for its carrying on this type of work.

The New Testament, however, never thinks of the Christian as primarily a citizen of a state. "Our commonwealth [or citizenship] is in heaven," as St Paul reminds the citizens of the Roman colony of Philippi (Phil. III.20), and it is only in heaven, with our bodies transformed to their true spiritual substance, and with all things in heaven and earth completely subject to Christ, that we shall be members of a state (if we can call that a state) to which we can give the whole-hearted allegiance of Zealots. The Christian "is the citizen of another Kingdom, and it is thence that he derives his way of thinking, judging and feeling. . . . He may be in this world, it is true, but all his 'ties' are elsewhere; all his ties of thought, truth and fidelity depend on the Lord, and he owes no allegiance to the world."[5] The emphasis of the Iona Community and other modern movements on Christians playing their full part in politics needs some qualification here. The Christian will never be a very good party man; his true citizenship is in heaven, and there will always be a certain detachment and a qualified appreciation in his attitude to the best-laid political schemes.

§ 2

As a second view of the state, much of the Old Testament gives a more realistic picture of the state as it is. In one account of Saul's elevation to the throne, Samuel describes the tyranny and oppression that would inevitably characterise the reign of an earthly king (1 Sam. VIII.10-17), and many prophets denounced the misdeeds of both their own and neighbouring kings. "The 'rulers' and 'judges' of the nations are particularly subject to divine judgment, because they oppress the poor and defy the divine Majesty."[6] On this view the state belongs to

[5] Ellul, *Presence*, p. 45 f.
[6] Niebuhr, *Nature and Destiny of Man*, VOL. II, p. 279.

the present evil order, and may indeed be necessary in order to keep the evils of this order in check. God uses the projects, even the wicked projects, of tyrants like the kings of Assyria and Babylon, to play a part in His purposes of good, but He will cast them aside when He is done with them. This Biblical view shares some truth with the Communist view of "the withering away of the state,"[7] but on the whole the Bible realises the positive value of the state more clearly than Communism does. St Paul saw, like the ancient prophets, that the Roman authorities were also instruments of the wrath of God, but he saw more in them than that.

The classical passage in St Paul is Rom. XIII.1-7, but the teaching given in the Pastoral Epistles (1 Tim. II.1-2; Tit. III.1-2) and 1 Peter (II.13-17) is so similar that we must believe that the Romans passage gives generally accepted apostolic teaching on the matter. We should probably give a very limited weight to considerations which may have biased St Paul in favour of the Roman state. He was a Roman citizen and proud of it. Like St Luke, both his own temperament and political prudence may have led him to see the best side of Roman rule. Rightly or wrongly, the Christians, who had originally been regarded as Zealots, were now suspected of being secret political agitators. Nero would not have tried to throw the blame for the fire in Rome on the Christians unless people had been ready to believe that this was the kind of thing Christians were likely to do. It was up to St Paul to show in his teaching how different the Christian attitude really was.

What then was St Paul's teaching?

1. St Paul saw the state as an institution appointed by God, perhaps not in the original plan of creation, but certainly to meet the needs of a fallen world as an instrument of God's wrath, which is His reaction to evil, at the same time inexorable and personal.[8] The order maintained by governments is in some measure an expression in this fallen world of God's own order. Cullmann's conviction that the word "authorities"

---

[7] V. Lenin, *The State and Revolution*, London 1919, p. 64.
[8] See p. 70.

(always used in secular literature for earthly governments, but always used by St Paul for spiritual powers), must include supernatural beings as well as human rulers, reminds us that there is a mystique in government, to which, other things being equal, a certain reverence is due. A king or government, even the Roman *imperium*, does not obtain its power either from purely natural causes or from a social contract or the like, but from God; older Jewish teachers had held this view (e.g. Wis. vi.3). It is unlikely that St Paul would have developed this teaching in the way it was developed by supporters of the divine right of kings, or even by some of the Reformers. John Knox gives what is surely the reasonable interpretation of this passage. "The power in that place is nocht to be understande of the unjuste commandiment of men but of the just power whairwith God hes armit his Magistratis and Lievtanantis to punische syn."[9] To decide whether rulers are over-reaching their God-given authority is, according to Knox, a task for "the wisdome and dicretioun of godlie subjectis."[10] The Church cannot escape this responsibility even in the modern world, although St Paul would rightly advise us to be slow to exercise it.

2. St Paul saw that the Roman authorities were actually checking wrongdoing, and in some measure encouraging morality. It may be that "he who restrains the mystery of lawlessness" in II Thess. ii.7 is the Roman Emperor, although cautious scholars hold that this is "not proven." To some extent even thoroughly bad and tyrannical governments are "a terror to evil-doers." Even in Nazi Germany, thieves and murderers in a non-political way found themselves in prison, and people who did real public service were commended so long as they did not deviate openly from the party line. A bad government may appear to the Christian a lesser evil than no government at all.

3. There is an implicit limitation of the functions of the state suggested in Rom. xiii.6: "For the same reason you also pay taxes, for the authorities are ministers of God attending to this very thing." "This very thing," in normal Greek

---

[9] J. Knox, *History of the Reformation in Scotland*, in *Works of John Knox*, ed. D. Laing, 6 vols., Edinburgh 1848, VOL. II, p. 437.

[10] *Op. cit.*, p. 440.

G

construction, would refer here to tax-gathering, but many translators, like Moffatt and J. B. Phillips, think that it must refer to the law and order indicated in the earlier verses. This does not seem necessary. Ezekiel had thought of the prince as primarily the raiser of temple revenues (Ezek. XLVI). The sphere of the things that are Caesar's is characteristically the raising of taxes and the expenditure of the money so raised; Budget Day is the high day of the Parliamentary year. St Paul sums up our Christian duty in the matter in the next verse, which may echo our Lord's similar teaching, by enjoining the payment of taxes and the like in order to carry on the work of government, and the showing of a fitting respect to rulers who are λειτουργοί or ministers of God in this rather strange sphere. To enjoin such respect in general does not imply that all rulers do God's will and deserve to be obeyed, any more than an injunction to give the customary respect to priests means that such degenerates as the sons of Eli are doing right and are worthy of respect.

St Paul is here one-sidedly emphasising certain truths about the state—perhaps those which Christians in Rome needed to learn. He had, however, other insights in this connexion. In I Cor. II.8 he refers to the rulers of this age having failed to understand the Christian revelation; otherwise they would not have crucified the Lord of glory. (Rulers (ἄρχοντες) here has the same ambiguity either earthly kings or heavenly powers as authorities (ἐξουσίαι) in Rom. XIII). This corresponds to our Lord's saying on the Cross; "Father, forgive them; for they know not what they do" (Lk. XXIII.34). This must still determine our attitude to governments who so often show misunderstanding of the real nature of the Gospel, for example in regarding the Church merely as a not too efficient booster of public morale or an underpaid ancillary to the state youth service. In I Cor. VI.1-6, St Paul reproves Christians for taking their disputes to the civil courts before the "unrighteous." He is not questioning the authority or justice of these courts. His point is that these courts belong to one order, the order of the fallen world where retribution is primarily the just way of dealing with wrongs, while Christians belong to another order, the order of the Kingdom of God, which is characterised by forgiveness and the patient enduring of wrongs. The modern

Christian who takes his case to a civil court is accepting the world's standards and not the standards of Christ; the case where two parties in good will refer a difficult matter to a court for decision is obviously an exception. St Peter has more to say on the Christian enduring wrongs patiently instead of asserting his rights (1 Pet. II.13-25); this is surely still one of the most striking ways in which the Christian style of life is different from that of the world. In 1 Tim. II.1-2 there is an exhortation to give thanks and to pray for the Roman authorities; this was in accordance with Jewish custom, and Christians had reason to be thankful for the law and order established by Rome, however much they might disapprove of much that went on in Caesar's household. It is possible with good reason to give thanks and pray for our own Royal Family without approving of their interest in horse-racing. In 1 Pet. II.16 the point is made that Christian freedom is not to be made an excuse for failing to meet the moral obligations demanded by the state. The likelihood that some Christians were interpreting their freedom in this way goes far to explain the New Testament emphasis on submission to civil authority.

§ 3

In Revelation we have a very different picture of the Roman authority from that of St Paul. In Romans the state appears as God's servant entrusted with the maintenance of law and order; in Rev. XIII the Roman state appears as the slave of Satan. The dragon, Satan, who had once offered on his own conditions the kingdoms of this world to Jesus, now gives his power over to the beast that is Rome, and men do just what Jesus refused to do—they worship the beast.[11] All do this, except the elect, in the great apostasy (Rev. XIII.8). The identification of the second beast, which appears in later passages (Rev. XVI.13, XIX.20, XX.10) to be the same as the false prophet, is more doubtful. Cullmann, influenced perhaps by the experience of our own propaganda-ridden age, thinks that it represents "the religio-ideological propaganda authority of the totalitarian state."[12] All this corresponds, if due

[11] Cullmann, *State in N.T.*, pp. 73 ff.
[12] *Op. cit.*, p. 76.

account is taken of apocalyptic flights of fancy, to the historical fact that the demand for Emperor-worship was the crisis at which the Roman state exceeded the God-appointed limits of its power by claiming authority over the souls of men as well as over their property and over public decency.   The Christian could not offer incense to Caesar even as a symbol of political loyalty; Christians in Manchuria in our own day similarly refused to worship the Emperor of Japan, although they were assured that it was merely a political symbol.   The modern state, in the free world at any rate, is likely to over-reach its powers in more subtle ways, in the control it exercises over education or over communication, for example, and constant vigilance is needed on the part of Christians.   The Roman power perhaps reached its lowest ebb as the provider of bread and circuses for a greedy proletariat, and a modern state can very easily go beyond its sphere in this direction also.

The Christian must refuse to obey the commands of a government over-reaching its authority.   This was all that the early Christians—a minority in a world empire—could do, and some of them suffered martyrdom for it.   In modern conditions can Christians do anything more?   They certainly can speak out against such a power, something that the writer of Revelation could only do in cryptic language such as that referring to Rome as Babylon.   Christians then knew what we can still know today, that a state like Rome was bound to experience the wrath of God in its full destructive power, quite apart from any resistance made by Christians.   It would seem reasonable that any Christian today who accepts the Catholic view that he can rightly bear arms in a just war between nations, should also take an active part in a just political revolt, although the New Testament gives no direct guidance here. Christians in Hungary in 1956 could neglect Romans XIII with good conscience.

§ 4

Our Lord Himself, in spite of the attractions of Zealot policy, remained aloof from the whole political set-up of the time.   On one occasion Jesus talked of Herod Antipas as "that fox" (Lk. XIII.32) in the same spirit as Revelation talked of Rome as "the mother of harlots" (Rev. XVII.1, 5), but at the same

time He was unusually friendly with the publicans, the collaborationists of the time, and He was more concerned with their
honesty and readiness to make restitution than with their
relations to the Roman authorities (Lk. xix.8, 9).

The significant incident in this connexion is that in which
Pharisees and Herodians attempt to catch out Jesus by asking
the question; "Is it lawful to pay taxes to Caesar or not?"
(Mk. xii.13-17, etc.). If Jesus answered "No," He could be
reported as a Zealot revolutionary. If He answered "Yes,"
He would lose face with the crowd who had little use for
declared collaborationists. This, however, was what He did,
for the truth was far more important to Him than popularity;
but He did it in such a way as to bring His questioners into the
same collaborationist group as Himself. The State, He
declared, can make just demands, and one of them is for
revenue. The coin that had been produced with Caesar's
name and picture on it, which everybody used in their
ordinary business, clearly belonged to Caesar; it was due to
Caesar like the taxes and tolls of Romans xiii. The second
part of His answer; "Render to God the things that are God's,"
goes quite beyond the question asked, and declares that there
is a sphere where God and not Caesar is the master. This
sphere may not have been clear to Jesus' original hearers,
but it became very clear to those faced later with the demand
for Emperor-worship. Tertullian's comment is still the most apt;
"Give to God what is God's—His image in man, yourself."[13]

Still, it is true that this saying does not clearly delimit
for us what belongs to God and what belongs to Caesar. The
limits depend to some extent on circumstances; a state, for
example, which provides a Health Service may demand from
the individual a care of his body which in other circumstances
would only be a matter between the individual and God.
What Jesus definitely enjoined was the payment of taxes.
No one who enjoys the security and conveniences which an
organised government provides has the right to refuse to pay
his share of the cost of these things, however much he may
disagree with the government's general policy. Clifford and
the passive resisters to the Education Bill of 1902 may have
been right in holding that religious education is outside Caesar's

[13] Tertullian, *de Idololatria*, 15.

sphere, but their refusal to pay rates was an unscriptural method of resistance. The Christian must normally accept the authority of the state in his dealings in money; that should be easy for one whose mind is set on the things that are above, not on things of the earth (Col. III.2). We moderns often say that all that we have, including our money, belongs to God. St Paul would certainly agree but would insist that the state is God's minister in dealing with money matters.

The argument is often used that if the New Testament teaches submission to an alien, pagan government, our duty to submit without question to the government of our own "Christian" country is still more clear. This is true only in so far as a government under Christian influences is less likely to over-reach its powers and more likely to give a limited expression to the law of Christ in its legislation. Basically the state, even though, like America, it regards itself as a "good neighbour-state,"[14] still belongs to the old order. In it the necessary practice is still punishment for wrong and not forgiveness; its rulers, although they may like to call themselves "benefactors" (Lk. XXII.25) are still tempted to lord it over their subjects. At the same time ideals of service, justice, and mutual help do have a large place in the modern Welfare State, and they were inspired by the Gospel of Christ. It is no accident that St Paul, after enjoining his Roman readers to pay the dues recognised in the old order, goes on to speak of the love due to every man in the new order, where Christ, and not Caesar, is king (Rom. XIII.7-8).

Literature

O. CULLMANN, *The State in the New Testament*, London 1957.

R. NIEBUHR, *The Nature and Destiny of Man*, London 1943, VOL. II, pp. 279-94.

E. BRUNNER, *The Divine Imperative*, London 1937, chs. XXXVI and XXXVII.

L. H. MARSHALL, *The Challenge of New Testament Ethics*, London 1948, pp. 149-60, 343-9.

---

[14] L. H. Marshall, *The Challenge of New Testament Ethics*, henceforth cited as *N.T. Ethics*, London 1948, p. 156.

Chapter IX

The New Testament Attitude to Wealth

THE New Testament differs much from the Old Testament in its views on worldly prosperity. By and large, the Old Testament regards wealth as a good thing, a sign of God's favour and blessing and a reward given by Him for obedience and loyalty (e.g. Ps. 1.3). The Book of Job, after all its deep insights into human misfortune, ends with the faithful Job being rewarded by renewed wealth and prosperity. At the same time the Old Testament does condemn the sins into which the rich man too easily falls (Is. iii.14-16, v.8-12; Amos iv.1, v.11-12, vi.4-6, viii.4-6, etc.). In the New Testament there is no suggestion that wealth is a good thing, except perhaps in so far as it meets the necessities of life, which God provides for His people; "your heavenly Father knows that you need them all" (Mt. vi.32). Material wealth is rather something to be given away in order that a man may secure spiritual riches (Lk. vi.38, xii.33, 34). Of course the Old Testament attitude to wealth is the almost universal human attitude. Politicians today speak of doubling the standard of living, as if there were no question of its desirability, and most of us feel that we ourselves should be better of a little more money. We may even wonder whether the New Testament writers did not accept this common assumption, although for them it is overshadowed by their Master's teachings.

The danger of riches which is most clearly shown in the Old Testament, is that the rich oppress and exploit the poor; this is the social evil against which both the Deuteronomic Code and the prophets speak most strongly. It is an extraordinary fact that, except in the epistle of James, this danger is ignored in the New Testament. James, indeed, saw this evil in all its horror. "Is it not the rich who oppress you, is it not they who drag you into court?" (Jas. ii.6). "Behold, the wages of the labourers who mowed your fields, which you kept back by fraud, cry out; and the cries of the harvesters have reached the ears of the Lord of hosts" (Jas. v.4). This is right in line with prophetic tradition, but there is nothing of it in the Pauline letters or directly in the Gospel. Our Lord found the danger of riches elsewhere.

In the Old Testament "usury," or the taking of interest on a loan, is condemned, although in Deuteronomy the condemnation is limited to the taking of interest from a fellow-Israelite (Dt. xxiii.19-20). The one New Testament passage which has been interpreted in the same way really enjoins giving rather than lending, so that there is no question of interest at all (Lk. vi.32-5). The references to the taking of interest in the parables of the pounds and talents suggest that to do so was the accepted practice of the time, and our Lord did not condemn it. We may believe that our Lord saw that the morality of taking interest is something that depends on circumstances. "To take interest from money lent to a neighbour who is in need (which is the only kind of lending known in primitive society) is a different thing from deriving interest from money or credit given to someone who wants to make more money by it."[1] No one who has seen the usury exacted from Indian peasants by money-lenders can doubt the evil of interest in these circumstances, but the modern lending of money on interest to those who use it for productive purposes seems, at least in our present economic system, to be socially advantageous and a just reward for self-restraint in spending. It may be that in our capitalist society too large a share of the national wealth goes to paying for capital and too little goes to paying for labour, but this is not an issue with which the Bible directly deals.

Richardson thinks that by New Testament times the words "poor" and "rich" had come to have a religious and ethical content rather than an economic one.[2] In the Psalms, for example, the poor are the humble, godly people who trust in Yahweh, perhaps the Hasidim of Maccabean times. In the Gospels, the poor are simple, devout people like Simeon. The

---

[1] E. Brunner, *Christianity and Civilisation*, London 1949, VOL. II, p. 92.

[2] A. Richardson, "Poor," in *A Theological Word Book of the Bible*, London 1950, p. 168.

rich are wicked, not because of their riches, but because, like the Sadducee priests, they make wealth by such wrong means as the Temple market. While our Lord and His disciples may have included, as we all do, characteristics other than actual wealth and poverty in their mental images of the rich man and the poor man, the essential thing about the rich man in the Bible remains his wealth, and about the poor man his poverty. The one phrase with a different suggestion is the phrase "poor in spirit" in the Beatitudes in Matthew (v.3). Some regard this as a later softening of the more direct "Blessed are ye poor" of Luke (vi.20), but, even if, as I think probable, our Lord did use on some occasion the actual words "poor in spirit," they only indicate that our Lord looked to the heart, to the inner reality as well as the outward circumstances, of the poor man. To do so is characteristic of the whole of the fifth chapter of Matthew. The poor man, however, remains poor in fact as well as in spirit.

§ 2

The New Testament speaks out against riches in themselves much more definitely than the Old. Even a modern economist admits that "the New Testament and the constant tradition of the Christian Church warn us against riches. . . . We cannot dismiss the New Testament as lightly as would some, who seek to justify the riches of the modern world."[3] The *locus classicus* for such warning is Mark x.23-6. Jesus had bidden the man who sought to inherit eternal life to sell all that he had and give the proceeds to the poor. The man had gone away in sorrow, for he had great possessions; in his case at any rate his wealth was a barrier preventing his entrance to the kingdom of God. Jesus then said; "How hard will it be for those who have riches to enter the kingdom of God!" As the disciples were amazed at such a revolutionary idea, our Lord apparently again said; "How hard it is to enter the kingdom of God!" (The form, "How hard it is for those who trust in riches," does not occur in the best manuscript sources,[4] and is almost certainly a toning down by a later scribe who

---

[3] D. L. Munby, *Christianity and Economic Problems*, London 1956, p. 119.
[4] Omitted, e.g. in Codices ℵ and B.

shared the disciples' horror). Jesus went on to use the picturesque figure of a camel struggling through the eye of a needle to illustrate the rich man's predicament. The disciples, now completely flabbergasted, exclaim; "Then who can be saved?" Jesus answered; "With men it is impossible, but not with God." There is a miracle of grace by which rich men, like Joseph of Arimathea and Zacchaeus the publican, can be saved.

The Church has found the primary evil not in the possession of riches, but in the sin of avarice or covetousness which the New Testament certainly condemns (e.g. Lk. XII.15). Today avarice is scarcely regarded as a sin. Even Christian statesmen appeal chiefly to men's avarice in their election programmes, and encourage it by Premium Bonds, for one of the basically wrong things about gambling is that it is a powerful and insidious stimulus to avarice. The New Testament goes further, and sees that the mere possession of riches is likely to increase a man's avarice; but for the grace of God the rich man is an avaricious man building ever greater barns. We are all surprised at the man with double our own income still striving to add to his wealth, but the man with half our income probably feels the same surprise at our efforts. Experience affirms the assumption underlying the Gospel teaching that the more money a man has, the more likely is he to set his heart on making still more money. There are, of course, exceptions, but this is the general rule.

What makes avarice or covetousness a sin is that money takes the place of God in our lives, or, more accurately, the pursuit of money takes the place of the worship of God. Munby, the economist whom we have already quoted, puts it cautiously; "The Christian Church does not condemn the good things of this life, because they are good, but because they tend to set man apart from God, and distract him with things that seem to have value in themselves, though in the last resort they derive all their significance from God. The use of riches, as of all good things of this life, requires a nice balance not easy to achieve, and unlikely to be achieved by those insensitive to the dangers and attractions of this world."[5] There is nothing of this nice balance in the New Testament. Jesus said simply;

[5] Munby, *Christianity and Economic Problems*, p. 119.

"You cannot serve God and mammon" (Mt. vi.24), and the service is that familiar to the ancient world, the service of a full-time slave. St Paul describes covetousness as idolatry—the making of money into a god (Col. iii.5). Jesus was giving similar teaching in the difficult saying which follows the parable of the unjust steward; "Make friends for yourselves by means of unrighteous mammon, so that when it fails they may receive you into the eternal habitations" (Lk. xvi.9). Whatever else this means, it teaches that money is to be used as a means, and not as an end in itself (like the worship of God), and the whole parable indicates that it is a very questionable means. Other parables tell a similar story of religion being crowded out by the lures of wealth: the rich fool, who thought that bigger barns could give him everything; or Dives, who had no thought for poor Lazarus at his gate.

To serve mammon means to seek one's security in riches instead of in God, obviously the mistake of the rich fool. Our Lord tried to rid his followers of this illusion by pointing out the "deceitfulness of riches," so easily destroyed by moth and rust or removed by the common thief (Mt. vi.19-21). In similar spirit 1 Timothy (vi.17) speaks of men settting their hopes on *uncertain* riches rather than on God, and James echoes one of our Lord's sayings when he says; "Your riches have rotted, and your garments are moth-eaten. Your gold and silver are rusted, and their rust will be evidence against you" (Jas. v.2-3). Again in Revelation there is a picture of so great riches coming to nought in fallen Rome (Rev. xviii.17). This teaching should have been brought home to our own generation by the change in the value of the money so that what seemed an adequate provision for old age forty years ago is now quite insufficient for the barest needs. Jesus added to all this the more positive teaching that we can trust our heavenly Father for all we really require (Mt. vi.32). This does not mean that there is no need to work; the Bible, as we shall see later,[6] regards work as the normal lot of man. It does mean that there is no need to worry about the future; the cure for the anxiety neuroses which are so common in our time is neither a larger private bank balance nor heavier national insurance, but trust in God.

[6] See Chapter x.

The New Testament realises that the possession of wealth is likely to lead a man into other vices as well as avarice, and here it has more in common with the Old Testament. The deadly sins of lust, gluttony, and sloth are vices in which the poor man has less chance of indulging, and the higher standard of living in our own day increases the common man's temptations in these directions. This is the indication of the text mistranslated in the Authorised Version; "The love of money is the root of all evil" (i Tim. vi.10). In that form the text is obviously untrue; there is much evil that springs from human desires other than the love of money. A more correct translation would be; "The love of money is a root of all sorts of evil" (literally, "all evils"). The preceding verse is an adequate comment: "Those who desire to be rich fall into temptation, into a snare, into many senseless and hurtful desires that plunge men into ruin and destruction."

Even apart from such direct temptations to vice, the New Testament sees that the rich man's mind is apt to be filled with many interests which, even when innocent or perhaps good in themselves, leave little room for religion. "A man's life does not consist in the abundance of his possessions" (Lk. xii.15), as the rich man easily imagines. "The kingdom of God does not mean food and drink but righteousness and peace and joy in the Holy Spirit" (Rom. xiv.17). This is why the Christian needs deliberately to set his mind "on things that are above, not on things that are on earth" (Col. iii.2). This crowding out of Divine things by material interests is different from the deliberate pursuit of wealth or a misplaced trust in wealth, and seems to be the characteristic form of avarice today. Misers are not now so common, and the economic instabilities of our century have made us a little sceptical about the value of laying up goods for many years. Today, however, "the world is so full of a number of things" to be bought with money, that they leave no room in many minds for the unseen and eternal things of real spiritual value which money cannot buy. This power of preoccupying the whole of the mind is one thing that makes money into "filthy lucre." Money itself is not "filthy" or "base" as our English translations suggest. In the four places that this phrase occurs in the Authorised Version (i Tim. iii.3; Tit. 1.7, 11; i Pet. v.2), it refers to a fault or temptation in an officer of the Church; bishops and the like may find money occupying their minds to the exclusion of more important things, just like other people, and their gain becomes then a base gain, a disgrace to their office. Of course, if the money comes by questionable means, the gain is all the more base.

§ 3

What then does the New Testament tell us to do about money? In one case Jesus made it very clear that the only thing one particular man could rightly do was to sell all that he had and give the proceeds to the poor (Mk. x.17-22). Commentators rightly point out that this command was given not as a general exhortation, but in order to meet a particular spiritual need, and that with other people, the barrier which prevents their attainment of eternal life may be something entirely different from wealth. Yet, the common attitude to money and "never having had it so good" being what it is, God may well speak to some through this text today, as He did to St Francis in the thirteenth century with extraordinary results. After all this Jew's possessions would probably look a very moderate capital in the modern world.

If Jesus' saying, "Sell all that you have," is not to be taken as a general rule, Jesus did lay down a general rule which is much more demanding and heart-searching than the command to get rid of one's property. Almost the most frequently recorded saying of our Lord is to this effect; "If any man would come after me, let him deny himself and take up his cross and follow me" (Mk. VIII.34; Mt. x.38, XVI.24; Lk. IX.23, XIV.27; Jn. XII.25). Self-denial, as we shall see later,[7] does not mean, as is commonly supposed, doing without sweets or tobacco or putting an extra shilling in the collection. Self-denial is not doing without cosmetics; it is doing without self, which is a harder business. It is so partly because it means an entirely different outlook on the business of making money, with which we are concerned in this chapter. Dorothy Sayers once put this very strikingly in a lecture: "The Church says Covetousness is a deadly sin—but does she really think so? Is she ready

[7] See Chapter XIV.

to found Welfare Societies to deal with financial immorality as she does with sexual immorality? Do the officials stationed at church doors in Italy to exclude women with bare arms turn anybody away on the grounds that they are too well-dressed to be honest? Do the vigilance committees who complain of 'suggestive' books and plays make any attempt to suppress the literature which 'suggests' that getting on in the world is the chief object in life? Is Dives, like Magdalen, ever refused the sacraments on the grounds that he, like her, is an 'open and notorious evil-liver'? Does the Church arrange services, with brighter congregational singing, for Total Abstainers from Usury?"[8] Of course this does not mean that we should use the same methods to combat covetousness as have been used in the battle against sexual vice and drunkenness. What it does mean is that our attitude to avarice should be more like the prevailing Christian attitude to these notorious evils. "Getting on in the world," means for too many Christians the making of more money, whereas, on any Christian standard, it should mean the giving of greater and more selfless service. There is no short-cut in the Christian life here; the only way to deal with covetousness is the complete change of heart which God alone can give.

§ 4

The modern world finds Christian teaching on stewardship— the prudent and generous use of material possessions—much more congenial than teaching on self-denial. The doctrine of Christian stewardship has found its Biblical authority largely in the older interpretations of such parables as those of the pounds and talents: the more modern interpretations given by Dodd and Jeremias make it doubtful whether we can still draw lessons about the Christian stewardship of money from them. It is, of course, true, if a little platitudinous, to maintain that everything we have, including our money, is a trust from God for which we are responsible. The most relevant and most difficult parable in this connexion is the story of the unjust steward (Lk. xvi.1-15). The sayings of our Lord which follow this story suggest two or three different lessons from it,

---

[8] D. L. Sayers, *The Other Six Deadly Sins*, London 1943, p. 15.

but no one supposes that the steward, when forging bills and falsifying his master's account-books, was in every respect an example to Christians in their dealings with money. One lesson, as we have already seen, is that money is to be regarded as a means and not as an end in the Christian life. Another lesson is that we should be good stewards of our spiritual heritage, which our Lord here calls "the true riches," and give to our Master as whole-hearted a devotion as the worldly give to their master Mammon. A third saying is more directly concerned with stewardship; "If then you have not been faithful in the unrighteous mammon, who will entrust to you the true riches?" The New Testament is too conscious of the moral ambiguities of money to make of it the sacred trust that some preachers on Christian stewardship have made it; "unrighteous mammon" is elsewhere "filthy lucre" and a root of all sorts of evil. What this parable teaches is that faithful service to an earthly master, including an honest handling of money, is required of the man who serves a heavenly Master. This is closely akin to the teaching given to slaves in the Epistles (Eph. vi.5-8; Col. iii.22-5). Jesus went on to reaffirm the principle given in another context in the Sermon on the Mount; "You cannot serve God and mammon," and the money-loving Pharisees scorned him for it. Stewardship of money is a subordinate, although genuine, element in Christ's teaching. By and large, St Paul takes the same position; it is responsibility in all personal relationships rather than the stewardship of money, which is emphasised in teachings on duties within the household. Our Lord accepted and enjoined on His followers the traditional Jewish duty of almsgiving, and St Paul was even more explicit about it. He suggested the weekly allotment of a regular sum (i Cor. xvi.2), and used the sublime example of our Lord becoming poor at His incarnation as an inspiration to generous giving (ii Cor. viii.9).

There is, undoubtedly, in many of our Churches today, an over-emphasis on finance. We can well understand the factors causing it—the greatly increased cost of carrying on Christian work, the lag in people adjusting the amount they give to the changed value of money, and the wholly Christian determination that religion should penetrate the whole of men's lives. Yet the New Testament way of speaking about money must make us distrust Christian campaigns which have the raising of money as their primary object, still more those which use high, spiritual teachings as a rather thinly disguised means to increase the income of the Church. Our Lord says to His Church as He says to individuals; "Seek first his kingdom and his righteousness, and all these things shall be yours as well" (Mt. vi.33).

§ 5

Max Weber was the first to expound a theory that there is a causal connexion between Calvinism and capitalism;[9] this is relevant to our subject only so far as we hold Calvinism to be a true development of New Testament teaching. Here we must distinguish between the deliberate intention of a teaching and its accidental consequences. Calvinism did emphasise the virtues of self-discipline and self-restraint and had New Testament authority for it (e.g. 1 Cor. ix.27), and in the capitalist ordering of society these virtues do lead to an increase of material resources not used up in ordinary consumption but available for use in further production, and this is just what is meant by capital. Some Quakers, with little in common theologically with the Calvinists except the will to take New Testament teaching seriously, also accumulated considerable wealth. Christ's command; "Do not lay up for yourselves treasures on earth," makes no distinction between wealth expended and wealth saved, and the emphasis of His teaching is against taking anxious thought for the morrow, which is one of the chief motives encouraging men to save. The Christian virtues of self-restraint in spending and of diligence in business were probably made too much of by some Calvinists; and it would be altogether contrary to New Testament teaching to suppose that Christians should practise them for the sake of the wealth to which they may lead. It is not in order to serve mammon that we serve God.

In contrast to those who link capitalism to Christian teaching there are some who think that the inevitable outcome of our Lord's teaching is a Christian Communism such as was

---

[9] M. Weber, *The Protestant Ethic and the Spirit of Capitalism*, London 1930. Translation of *Gesammelte Aufsätze zur Religionssoziologie*, Tübingen 1922, I, pp. 89 ff.

practised in the early Jerusalem Church (Acts IV.32-7). To take part in this experiment was entirely voluntary; Barnabas is mentioned as a noteworthy example of those who did so, and the fault of Ananias and Sapphira was not in refusing to join the community, but in deceiving the community as to what they were doing (Acts v.3-5), something that would necessarily break down the mutual trust which is essential for such voluntary communism. The experiment may have made too much of the material at the expense of the spiritual, but it was a noble and idealistic expression of the fellowship of believers. The Christian ethic, however, is always realistic as well as idealistic, and when because of the hardness of men's hearts this voluntary communism did not work, it was given up, and has never since been attempted by the Catholic Church. Its lesson for the Church today is not that we should repeat this particular experiment, but that we should be trying new experiments in the way of expressing our unity in Christ, like the Iona Community or the "Jesus Family" in Communist China.

§ 6

The New Testament attitude to wealth is certainly a good deal more critical than that of most Christians today. Yet the Bible never says that wealth is evil in itself; money is "filthy lucre" only when it is gained or used basely. After all wealth consists ultimately not in coin or paper token, but in God's good gifts in nature, and who dare call these evil in themselves? Wealth, at least in a fallen world, must be held and used by men in some way or other. Christians should not only plan for better ways of dealing with finance on their frontier with the economists; they should also be very sensitive to the danger to themselves as individuals of holding too great a share of the world's wealth. The common and the modern Socialist view finds the essence of this danger in the depriving other people of their fair share. The New Testament finds a greater danger in earthly things taking the place of heavenly things in the rich man's heart. And here the rich man with whom we are primarily concerned is always our own self!

H

Literature

A. RICHARDSON, "Poor," in *A Theological Word Book of the Bible*, London 1955.

E. BRUNNER, *Christianity and Civilisation*, London 1949, VOL. II, ch. VII.

D. L. MUNBY, *Christianity and Economic Problems*, London 1956, esp. ch. VI.

M. WEBER, *The Protestant Ethic and the Spirit of Capitalism*, London 1930. Translation of "Die protestantiche Ethik und der Geist des Kapitalismus," in *Gesammelte Aufsätze zur Religionssoziologie*, Tübingen 1922. I, pp. 89 ff.

Chapter X

The New Testament Attitude to Work

THE word "work" appears in the Bible in three principal connexions. There is, first of all, the work of God, seen chiefly in creation, but also, according to John, in the activities of life-giving and judgment in which our Lord shared. We moderns like to think that creativity is one respect in which man was made in God's image, but there is no hint of this in Scripture, which emphasises man's creatureliness rather than his creative power. The Hebrews, indeed, distrusted human works of art as involving idolatry. There is one noteworthy exception to the common attitude of the Bible; a craftsman engaged in the making of furnishings for the Tabernacle is described as "filled with the Spirit of God" because of his exceptional gifts (Ex. xxxv.31). Allegorists have commonly regarded the talents of the parable, which are literally large sums of money, as representing our human capacities, and it is from this parable that the English meaning of talent as a capacity is derived. Such talents are certainly God-given and include the power to create poetry, music, and other works of art. St Paul's exhortation to his readers to think about things that are lovely and gracious and worthy of praise (Phil. iv.8) is the nearest that the New Testament comes to an explicit appreciation of art, although it is implicit in much of the imagery of Revelation. We may believe that our modern emphasis on creative activity is a true development of that truth into which the Holy Spirit leads Christ's followers.

§ 2

Work in the New Testament is commonly work for the cause of the Gospel, what we should call "Christian work" or "Church work" or even "good works," as contrasted with the work by which men earn their living. Our Lord exhorted His disciples;

"Do not labour for the food which perishes, but for the food which endures to eternal life," and later in explanation: "This is the work of God, that you believe in him whom he has sent" (Jn. vi.27, 29). St Paul bade his readers; "Work out your own salvation with fear and trembling; for God is at work in you, both to will and to work for his good pleasure" (Phil. ii.12-13). In this way men become "fellow workmen for God" (i Cor. iii.9), "working together with him" (ii Cor. vi.1). Similarly St Paul remembered with gratitude the Thessalonians' "work of faith and labour of love." (i Thess. 1.3).

It is evident from these and other New Testament passages that according to it the business of life is, first and foremost, the salvation of men, both other people and ourselves. The present-day tendency in secular life to make economic progress man's chief end, and the more insidious danger of regarding Christian work as primarily social service, are both contrary to New Testament teaching. These things may be good in a secondary way, but the great work of man is to glorify God by receiving the salvation He gives, and by working it out in life.

Again, while vocation—the fact of our being called by God —is a characteristically New Testament notion, it is not used there, as in our modern speech, with regard to our ordinary daily work. In the New Testament men are called to be saints or apostles or fishers of men; they are not called to be doctors or teachers or carpenters. The Reformers used the word "vocation" for a man's weekday occupation as a protest against the medieval tendency to limit the idea of vocation to those called to a monastic life, and they were of course right that a man can serve God as doctor or artisan as well as priest or monk. When St Paul tells new Christians that everyone should remain in the calling in which he was called,[1] the noun "calling" does not, I believe, refer, as Richardson suggests, to "the calling of God, by which he was brought out of heathen darkness into the light of the truth,"[2] but neither does it refer primarily to a man's secular occupation. The context suggests that it refers to his status as slave or freedman, and perhaps

---

[1] i Cor. vii.20 The R.S.V. translation of κλῆσις as "state" conceals the double use of the root meaning "call" in the original Greek.

[2] A. Richardson, *The Biblical Doctrine of Work*, henceforth cited as *Work*, Ecumenical Biblical Studies vol. i, London 1952, p. 36. (This is a book to which I owe much in this chapter.)

also incidentally to his status as married or single. The Holy
Spirit may reasonably lead us to apply this teaching to a man's
occupation at the time of his conversion. The danger in the
Reformers' conception of vocation is that in our emphasis on all
honest work as being given by God as a vocation, we forget
that there are men called to distinctively Christian callings.
For example, while it is true that every Christian working in
a non-Christian environment has a duty to bear witness to
Christ in his work and his whole way of living, yet God still
calls men to a definitely missionary occupation, one that it
would be folly for any man to undertake without such a call
and one to which God still summons men whom the experts
regard as unsuitable and who may be deeply conscious of their
own unworthiness.

The varieties of this specifically Christian work in New
Testament times differ considerably from the varieties of
service found in the Church today. In Eph. iv.11 God's
special gifts were given to enable men to be apostles, prophets,
evangelists, pastors, and teachers. In a rather wider list in
1 Cor. xii.28. St Paul includes apostles, prophets, teachers,
workers of miracles, healers, helpers, administrators, and
speakers in various kinds of tongues. A third list in Rom.
xii.6-8 contains prophets, deacons (who may simply be
servants), teachers, counsellors, givers, administrators, and
people engaged in works of mercy. In these lists there is no
rigid or limited classification of church officers, such as ecclesiastical legalists still try to make, and under the conditions of
today St Paul might well have added to the list. There is little
to be said for confining the recognised orders of the Church
to ministers, elders, and deacons, or even to these with the
addition of bishops. St Paul's lists sound more realistic and,
at the same time, more imaginative. St Paul would have
regarded our modern church secretary and even the stoker of
the church boiler as called to Christian service; he would not
have so regarded the secretary in a commercial office or the
stoker in a factory, although he would have maintained that
these too are called to be saints and witnesses for Christ
equally with the Church's paid officials. St Paul certainly
never thought of Christian service as something limited to a
priesthood or ministry.

§ 3

What is ordinarily understood by work is all the things that men do "from ruling empires to hewing wood and drawing water," generally but not necessarily in order to earn their living. The Bible is realistic about such work, neither exalting it as some Victorian moralists did, nor despising it in the fashion of some of the ancient Greeks. In the Genesis story, man was given the task of subduing the earth (Gen. 1.28), and there must have been some tilling of the garden of Eden before the Fall. So, to put it in modern language, work is a part of the natural order of things. Human sin, however, led to the disturbance of this natural ordering of the whole of man's life, including his work, so that his labour became a misery. Both Old and New Testaments regard it as the normal lot of man to work while daylight lasts. "Man goes forth to his work and to his labour until the evening" (Ps. CIV.23), and then "night comes when no one can work" (Jn. IX.4). (This New Testament text is the sole Scriptural basis for the Victorian hymn, "Work for the night is coming," which certainly gives work an importance never given to it in the Bible.) The most striking statement of the place of work in the natural order is found in St Paul's exhortation to those Thessalonians who had given up their ordinary occupations in view of the immediacy of the expected return of our Lord; "If any one will not work, let him not eat" (II Thess. III.8-12). This looks like a proverb, but it may have been an original utterance of St Paul himself, who reinforced it by his own practice of working for his living. A very similar phrase occurs in the words of the Jewish Rabbi Hunna and elsewhere in Rabbinic literature.[3] This must not be taken as a prohibition of unemployment pay, for St Paul could not envisage our modern industrial situation. What St Paul is doing is to state the "natural law" in this connexion; all-round failure to work, as in a general strike, would still mean all-round starvation.

Richardson points out correctly that the nearest New Testament parallel to the working-man of today is the slave or δοῦλος.[4] In the ancient world most of what we should call work was

---

[3] C. J. Ellicott, *St. Paul's Epistles to the Thessalonians*, London 1866, p. 131.
[4] Richardson, *Work*, p. 41.

done by slaves. Some slaves were engaged in professions like medicine and teaching, and there are people today who forget that professional people are still workers. The parallel between a slave and a working-man fails in two respects. (*a*) A slave was the property of his master in a way that no working-man is today. Our Lord's statement that "no one can serve two masters" was a simple fact of the time rather than a moral injunction. The modern working-man is commonly for over a hundred and twenty hours a week his own master, unless he hires out his spare time to a second employer. (*b*) On the other hand the relationship between master and slave in households was a more personal, and potentially a more Christian relationship in New Testament times than the relationship between employers and men under modern industrial conditions. An illustration of this is that the fullest statement of the duties of workers in the New Testament occurs in what are called the "house-tables" in the Epistles (Eph. v.21-vi.9; Col. iii.18-iv.1; 1 Pet. ii.18-iii.7). Such tables may have come originally from Stoic and other popular moralists, but in the Christian Church they took a characteristic form, stating the duties of husbands and wives, parents and children, masters and slaves. The slave, of course, did not have the status of the child, as St Paul makes clear elsewhere (Gal. iv.1-2), but he was like a child in being a member of the household under the personal care and guidance of his master. This makes the slave-master relationship to some degree a fitting symbol for the relationship of the Christian to Christ. The hired labourer was also in existence in New Testament times; he is found in Zebedee's boat, in the home of the prodigal son, and in the market-place waiting to be hired. Although we know little about the hired labourers, they probably were more in the position of our modern casual labourers, while the slaves were more like those on the permanent establishment in a modern industrial or other concern.

What then is the New Testament teaching about our daily work?

1. Work is to be done well. In Colossians iii.23-4 we are told; "Whatever your task, work heartily as serving the Lord and not men; ... you are serving the Lord Christ"; and there is a similar exhortation in Ephesians vi.5-8. Our work is not

only a service to our particular master; it is a service to our fellow men, and one motive for doing honest work is that we may be able to help those in need (Eph. iv.28). In and through this service to our fellow men our work is a service to our real master, Christ. Work done for Him must be work into which we have put our best. So, in the Pastoral Epistles, one motive suggested for faithful work is that by it men "adorn the doctrine of God our Saviour" (Tit. ii.10), and another is "that the name of God and the teaching may not be defamed" (1 Tim. vi.1). A man may work, and work hard, simply in order to earn his living, but those who work in order to serve their fellows and to serve Christ will do work of a different quality. St Paul would agree thoroughly with our modern emphasis on the layman witnessing for Christ both by the goodness of his work and by his personal relationships in factory or business.

2. There is no sign whatever of the Greek contempt for manual labour, even if it be the work of a slave, in the New Testament. Our Lord Himself, according to one verse in Mark (vi.3), had done the work of an artisan, and St Paul may have had this in mind when he speaks of our Lord as taking the form of a slave (Phil. ii.7). St Paul himself worked with his hands as a tent-maker, and he valued the independence he gained through earning his living in this way, although it is difficult to be sure whether he was moved by personal pride or by Christian expediency. John the Baptist did not instruct his penitents to give up such occupations as tax-collecting and soldiering (Lk. iii.12-14), although it would be difficult to think of these occupations as doing service to God in the conditions of first-century Palestine; his hearers certainly had to refrain from the abuses which had brought these occupations into disrepute. Nor does the New Testament scorn the fact that it is for his living that a man needs to work. The use of the proverbial saying; "The labourer is worthy of his hire" (Lk. x.7; 1 Tim. v.18), both by our Lord and by St Paul, shows that to do so is part of the natural order of things, even when there are other and more specifically Christian motives inspiring a man to work.

The majority of people in New Testament times did not have much choice of occupation, even less so than the majority today, and there is little direct guidance in the New Testament as to the employments in which a Christian may engage. There are a few occupations which are immoral in themselves; St Paul wrote; "Let the thief no longer steal" (Eph. IV.28), and obviously the Christian cannot be a burglar or a prostitute or a hired assassin. At the other extreme there are, over and above distinctively religious vocations, occupations in which the very nature of the work seems to invite men to loving service of their fellow men after the example of Christ; such are the professions of the doctor, the nurse, and, less obviously, the teacher. There is the same possibility of a distinctively Christian service in many other occupations, for example those of the farmer, the factory-worker, the shop-assistant and the housewife, although in them the direct serving of one another in love (Gal. v.13) may not be so outwardly conspicuous. The occupations which a Christian may hesitate to enter are of at least three classes. (a) There are occupations in which what is provided to the public is likely to do positive harm in present conditions. The seller of arms at least in under-developed countries, the seller of alcoholic liquors in slum areas, and the canvasser for sales by hire-purchase in new housing areas are at present engaged in such occupations, although these might in other circumstances be useful services. (b) There are occupations, which, while not obviously doing positive harm, are not providing any useful service to society, such as the conducting of football pools (which some, like the present writer, would regard as definitely anti-social), or the production of the sillier kinds of popular literature. (c) There are occupations, permissible in themselves, into which a Christian should not enter because of some known weakness in his character. A man who is tempted to drink too much should avoid the licensed trade, or a man with homosexual tendencies should avoid the army or other occupations in which his society is likely to be largely limited to people of his own sex.

For most occupations what matters for the Christian is the way in which the occupation is carried out rather than the nature of the occupation itself. The actor may be a minister to the community's spiritual needs or a corrupter of public morals, according to the way that he uses his opportunities; the landlord of the inn may be the kindly host providing a healthy social life for his neighbours or the deliberate exploiter of human weakness for his own gain. We have already mentioned the New Testament emphasis on work well done, and of the two legitimate aims recognised in the New Testament—the earning of a living and the service of the community—the latter should always come first with the Christian. While it is clear that the Christian must refrain from cooking the books, even under his employer's orders, or from getting paid for work he has not done, or from lying to a customer, the Christian may find a right decision more difficult when he is bidden to sell shoddy goods, or goods that do not come up to the advertised standard. In most occupations there are conventional norms of what is and what is not done, some entirely good, others more questionable. The Christian completely refusing to accept these recognised standards would need to go out of the business or even, as St Paul said, out of the world altogether (1 Cor. v.9-10). In practice what is important is that the Christian should be a little ahead of these standards, and so play his part in raising them, even though this is likely to cause him personal difficulty or even loss of employment.

3. At the same time we do not find in the New Testament that exaltation of work as a moral duty, which has been perhaps too characteristic of the Calvinist and Puritan traditions. Man's chief end is not to "fill brightest hours with labour" any more than it is to serve mammon. Labouring for the food that perishes is something very secondary to labouring for the food which endures to eternal life (Jn. VI.27). *Laborare est orare* is by no means the teaching of the New Testament. When Ben Sirach says of artisans; "In the handywork of their craft is their prayer" (Ecclesiasticus XXXVIII.34), his meaning most probably is that their labour is the best service of which such artisans are capable; they would be better praying if they could. The strongest link between work and worship in the New Testament is its use of the Greek word λειτουργία and its cognates. This was used in Classical Greek for secular work in the form of public service given to the state, and in the Septuagint for the religious duties of priests. Similarly, St Paul refers to the rulers of the state as λειτουργοί (Rom. XIII.6), and uses the word λειτουργία for

the worship of the Church and its works of charity (II Cor.
IX.12; Phil. II.17, 30). Λειτουργία in the New Testament
never refers to the ordinary work of common men; it is because
the ruler of the state is God's specially appointed servant with
a task in the world somewhat analogous to that of the
minister in the Church that he is called a λειτουργός. The
glorifying of God in Christian worship and service comes
before ordinary work; we are to seek the kingdom of God and
His righteousness, and not to worry about our daily bread
(Mt. VI.33).

4. The New Testament, in agreement with the Fourth
Commandment, recognises the need of leisure. Our Lord's
teaching brings the Sabbath back to its original purpose as a
day of rest and recreation for toiling men; "the Sabbath was
made for man, not man for the sabbath" (Mk. II.27-8). The
accompanying saying; "The Son of man is lord even of the
sabbath" may imply also that the Sabbath is given as a day
for the worship of that Lord. Of course in the ancient world
the only days of leisure from work were holy days, as our
English word "holiday" indicates. There is in the natural
order of things, as symbolised in the days of Creation, a rhythm
of work and rest, and, less obviously, a rhythm of work and
worship. Under ideal conditions, a man may find his ordinary
daily work refreshing and recreative, just as he may find it a
form of worship and service to God, as the tag *laborare est
orare* bears witness, but the Bible is far too realistic to suggest
such things for a fallen world. To make the best of things
as they are, a man should have days of leisure as well as days of
work, and a man's worship should come before his work.
Christians should always put what pressure they can on the
government of the day to provide opportunities for increased
leisure and particularly for the worship of God; this, and not
the maintenance of Jewish taboos, appears to be the Christian
ground for seeking that the Lord's day should be a peaceful
and recreative holiday for all.[5] In the New Testament rest
is spoken of as the proper culmination of man's work on earth.
In Hebrews IV God's rest on the seventh day of creation, the
rest of the Hebrew settlement in Palestine, and the rest that

[5] See W. Lillie, *The Law of Christ*, ch. VIII, "The Hallowing of Sunday," for a
treatment of this subject by the writer of this book.

remains for the people of God in heaven are all brought under one pattern. St Paul saw in the life of the resurrection the assurance that our labour (possibly our Christian service) is not in vain in the Lord (1 Cor. xv.58), and in Revelation their works follow those who die in the Lord (Rev. xiv.13). In these passages, the rest that is our human goal is no mere negative abstention from the work of earth, but a fuller recreated life where man's activity finds a new meaning and accomplishment.

5. In the house-tables the relationship of slave to master is always described as one of subordination. It is the duty of the slave to be obedient "with fear and trembling" (Eph. vi.5), to obey "in singleness of heart" (Col. iii.22), to "regard their masters as worthy of all honour" (1 Tim. vi.1), and "to be submissive . . . and give satisfaction in every respect" (Tit. ii.9). St Peter even expects slaves who do right and suffer for it to take their suffering patiently (1 Pet. ii.20). These were certainly prudent counsels of expediency for Christians who were slaves with scarcely any recognised legal rights in the Roman empire. Their place in Scripture suggests that they are also universally valid counsels, requiring of course modifications appropriate to the circumstances of workers in different social conditions. In every economic system, domestic, feudal, capitalistic, and communistic, there are those who direct and instruct on the one hand, and those who obey and carry out instructions on the other, and the counsels of the house-tables still speak to Christian managers and employees. Even today, almost everybody has some kind of master if not "too many masters," and St Paul would certainly remind those who have no earthly master that they have a Master in heaven. Such people have a very special responsibility to seek and to obey the direct guidance of God, and the Church should be constantly reminding the leaders in politics and business of this responsibility.

St Peter in the same context appears to hold that the undeserved hardships of slaves have a positive value in religion, inasmuch as these slaves are sharing in the sufferings of Christ, who "when he was reviled . . . did not revile in return . . . but trusted to him who judges justly" (1 Pet. ii.23). Is this to be taken as guidance for the modern Christian worker to bear the unjust treatment of himself and his mates without protest?

Should such a Christian worker refuse to take part in a strike the success of which might mean the end of certain of his sufferings? There is one significant difference between ancient slavery and modern employment. The slaves to whom St Peter was writing had generally to suffer willy-nilly; there was normally no way of escaping an unjust beating. What mattered in such circumstances was the spirit in which the sufferings were endured, and it made all the difference to that spirit if Christian slaves realised that they were sharing in the sufferings of Christ. (This realisation had the same importance for those Christians of our own time who suffered in prisons and concentration camps.) There is nothing, however, in the New Testament to suggest that Christians should deliberately seek suffering for themselves any more than Jesus Himself did so (Mk. xiv.36, etc.), or that they should by their submission help to perpetuate wrongs done to their fellow workers as well as to themselves. The Christian worker today has the power, by sharing in a strike or by other action within his trade union, to do something towards removing wrongs, and his Christian decision may be that this is the right thing to do for the sake of his fellow workers. What the New Testament does suggest is that in a complicated situation—and industrial disputes today are often very complicated—the Christian will, other things being equal, favour submission rather than active resistance; the Christian resisting authority must always be very sure of his ground. The modern worker's power to resist means that he has also a power in peace-making that the first-century slave did not have, and the Christian should be a peace-maker. As we have already suggested, there was one respect in which first-century relations between masters and men at least in domestic employment were better than our own, and the greatest need, from the Christian point of view, in modern industry is the recovery by every possible means of those personal relationships which the New Testament writers take for granted as existing between masters and slaves in their homes. Only thus will the teachings of the house-tables be directly applicable today.

In other problems confronting the Christian trade unionist today, such as restrictive practices, the closed shop, or sending men to Coventry, the situation is often so complicated and so concerned with technical matters that it is difficult to find any direct guidance in the New Testament, and the Christian moralist can only give counsel in the most general terms. What is important is that the Christian should exercise the freedom to which he is called in Christ and not accept unthinkingly and in sheep-like fashion the practices of his union. What should determine the Christian's vote, which, of course it is his duty to use, is not his own self-interest, but consideration of others, certainly of his own fellow workers within the union, but also of men of other unions, who may be thrown out of work or otherwise injured by his union's action, of his employers, and of the general public served by his trade. These various interests may well pull in different directions, and a truly Christian decision can only be made after much thought and prayer in each particular case.

§ 4

After reviewing all that the New Testament has to say about work, we must admit that it does not give to work the import-ance given to it by modern statesmen or modern moralists or even most conscientious Christians in their ordinary lives. The Sermon on the Mount is more concerned with what a man is than with what a man does, and the Johannine writings, which emphasise the work of God in us and for us, are more concerned with life and love than with work and accomplish-ment. The modern world makes the assumption that by plans of action, whether they be five-year plans or fifty-year plans, it can build the Kingdom of Heaven on earth, and, if this were the case, everything would depend on work—the work of the labourer as well as of the planner. Christians, of course, share with the modern planner the vision of the city that is to be, but they know that it must "come down out of heaven from God" (Rev. xxi.2). Men do have their place in the coming kingdom as "fellow workmen for God," but the New Testament is here thinking more of their Christian work and witness than of their daily occupation. "That men should be *alive*, instead of being obsessed with action," is part of Jacques Ellul's plea for a Christian style of life today. We think of Christian action "in the rational form of mechanical means. We no longer conceive it in the form which is constantly suggested in the Scriptures: the corn which *grows*, the leaven at work within the bread, the light which banishes the darkness. . . . In a civilisation which has lost the meaning of life, the most useful thing a Christian can do is to *live*."[6]

Such living will indeed include work, although it will not give work the first place. Yet the fact that the Bible uses the word "work" for God's own activity suggests that work has a sacramental aspect. Man's control over nature, authorised by Divine command in the Creation story (Gen. 1.28) and so marvellously realised through the techniques of modern science, is connected with man having been made in the image of God. Again man's fellowship in work, which should be the Christian consequence of the division of labour, is a symbol of, and may be a preparation for, the communion of the saints. Again the products of men's labour making use of God's natural gifts—bread and wine—are the symbols appointed by Christ for His work of redemption.[7] It is as we realise these things that our ordinary work will find its true place in a life that is more than work, a life in which worship comes before work. It is a common modern cliché that our worship must be made relevant to our work. It would be truer to the New Testament to say that our work should be made relevant to our worship, for the Kingdom of God and His righteousness are what must always come first.

Literature

A. RICHARDSON, *The Biblical Doctrine of Work*, Ecumenical Biblical Studies
 VOL. I, London 1952.
L. H. MARSHALL, *The Challenge of New Testament Ethics*, London 1948,
 pp. 341-3.
E. BRUNNER, *Christianity and Civilisation*, London 1949, VOL. II, pp. 72-85.
J. ELLUL, *The Presence of the Kingdom*, London 1951. Translation of *Présence
 au monde moderne*, Geneva 1948.

[6] Ellul, *Presence*, p. 93 f.
[7] Richardson, *Work*, pp. 71-6.

Chapter XI

The New Testament Attitude
to Marriage and Divorce [1]

THE teaching of our Lord on marriage and divorce must be considered in the light of Jewish practice at the time. Our knowledge of such practice is largely derived from the Mishna, the collection of Jewish laws arranged under topics about A.D. 200, and from later commentaries. Apart from certain groups, like some of the Essenes, who held more rigorous views, the vast majority of Jews at the time of Christ probably followed the practices later described in the Mishna.

R. Yaron has pointed out the confusion that occurs in the study of Jewish practice from failure to distinguish between what a man may *lawfully* do and what a man *ought* to do. Today in Britain the fact that a man may lawfully divorce his wife on certain grounds does not mean that he ought to divorce her. Generally speaking a Jew could lawfully divorce his wife without having any ground for doing so. This freedom was limited in two ways. (*a*) A man could not divorce a wife whom he had accused falsely of unchastity before her marriage or a wife whom he had been forced to marry after ravishing her (Deut. xxii). (*b*) A man had to pay his divorced wife a sum of money promised in the marriage contract. The frequently quoted passage from the Mishna is not concerned with what a man may lawfully do but with what a man ought to do. The school of Shammai held that a man *ought not* to divorce his

---

[1] I owe much in this chapter to the discussions of the Church of Scotland Special Committee on the Remarriage of Divorced Persons, of which I was a member, and particularly to three papers given as appendixes to the 1957 report of the Committee (henceforth cited as *C. of S. Report on Remarriage,* 1957) by Dr R. Yaron, Principal M. Black, and the late Professor W. Manson. I had also some talk with Dr Yaron on this matter.

wife unless she has been guilty of unchastity, while the school of Hillel held that he *may* divorce his wife if she has spoiled a dish in cooking, or even if he has found another fairer woman to be his wife. Even the school of Shammai would have had to admit that such easy divorces were legal, however undesirable.[2]

Among Jews divorce was a private legal act and did not require the decision of a court as in our modern practice. Matthew was describing Jewish practice accurately when he wrote; "Joseph was minded to put her away privily" (Mt. 1.19, A.V.). While a husband had legal freedom to put away his wife without reason, people might disapprove of his doing so. R. Johanan says; "He that sends away his wife is hated," and R. Eleazar says; "If a man divorces his first wife the altar sheds tears."[3] A wife had no right of divorce, but if her husband were engaged in certain trades, for example that of a coppersmith or of a tanner, or if he suffered from certain diseases, such as boils, she could apply to the court, which might decide that the husband should divorce her.[4] It is still the husband, and not the court, who delivers the bill of divorce. In the Gentile world things were different, and this may explain a New Testament reference to a wife divorcing her husband (Mk. x.12). Herodias was un-Jewish enough to send her husband a bill of divorce dissolving the marriage, which, Josephus pointed out, was contrary to the laws of the Jews.[5] The Jewish wife has been protected by later legal developments, so that today Jewish divorce is commonly divorce by consent. This is contrary to those divorce laws made under Christian influence which do not permit divorce by mutual consent.

Jewish divorce made the remarriage of the wife possible; the essential formula of the bill of divorce was; "Lo, thou art free to marry any man." This was subject to the two limitations that a priest could not marry a divorced woman (Lev. XXI.7, 14), and that a man could not marry his own former wife, if in the meantime she had been married to another

[2] Gittin 9.10, from *The Mishna*, ed. H. Danby, London and Oxford 1933, p. 321.
[3] Gittin 90*b*, from *The Babylonian Talmud, Gittin*, ed. M. Simon, London 1936, p. 439.
[4] Ketuboth 7.10, from *The Mishna*, ed. Danby, p. 255.
[5] Flavius Josephus, *De Antiquitatibus iudaicis*, Bk. XVIII, ch. v, §4.

I

(Dt. xxiv.4). Here again there was much Rabbinic counsel on the folly of marrying a divorced woman, although it was legal to do so.[6] In view of contemporary Jewish practice, it is extremely unlikely that early Christian teaching permitted divorce but forbade remarriage, as some have imagined.

In one respect the Jewish standard was more rigorous than our own and indeed than that of the prophet Hosea. A man was bound to divorce a wife guilty of adultery, and even if he were merely suspicious he ought to divorce her, although in that case he would have to pay the sum agreed in the marriage contract. A woman divorced because of adultery was forbidden to marry her lover, another provision that would interfere with one of the most common modern motives for seeking divorce.

Polygamy was permitted to Jews at the time of Christ; it was only abolished by a ruling in the eleventh century. There were Rabbis who recommended that a man should have only one wife at a time, and the "one flesh" passage in Genesis was a source of much difficulty to orthodox scholars in this connexion.[7] Economic conditions, however, probably discouraged polygamy even in New Testament times, so that the more widespread social evil then, as now, was divorce.

§ 2

Our Lord's fundamental teaching on divorce, given in Mk. x.2-9 and Mt. xix.2-8, is clear and decisive. Pharisees put Jesus to the test by asking him (according to Mark); "Is it lawful for a man to divorce his wife?" The affirmative answer to this question was so clearly given in Deuteronomy that we must suppose that the Pharisees already knew that Jesus was forbidding divorce. Some scholars consider that Matthew's form of the question; "Is it lawful to divorce one's wife for any cause?" is more likely to be original, because it raises the more vital issue disputed by the rival schools of Hillel and Shammai. This dispute may have influenced Matthew's language, but, as we have already seen, this dispute did not deal with what was *lawful*, and "lawful" is the word that occurs in both

[6] E.g. R. Judah ben Bathyra, quoted Daube, *N.T. and Rabbinic Judaism*, p. 77.
[7] *Op. cit.*, p. 81 f.

Gospels. In any case the Pharisees were not likely to have asked the question in a form that might rally the stricter school of Shammai to Jesus' support. The Pharisees, either in reply to a question by Jesus, or of their own accord at a later stage in the discussion, refer to the passage generally accepted as final in the matter, Dt. xxiv.1-4, which gives a man complete freedom to divorce his wife. Jesus declared that this concession had been made for their "hardness of heart," a spiritual condition which made it impossible for them to meet God's demands. At this point in Mark (and earlier in Matthew) Jesus, without directly contradicting Deuteronomy, quoted two other passages from the Torah with, presumably, equal authority; "From the beginning of creation, God made them male and female" (Gen. 1.27), and; "For this reason a man shall leave his father and mother and be joined to his wife, and the two shall become one" (Gen. 11.24). In both accounts Jesus added the comment; "So they are no longer two but one. What therefore God has joined together, let not man put asunder." The first of the two quotations from Genesis; "Male and female created he them," may appear to us irrelevant to the questions of monogamous marriage and divorce, but Daube has argued, in my opinion conclusively, that this verse was interpreted in our Lord's time in the light of the myth of the original androgynous man.[8] In simpler and more Scriptural terms, this is the doctrine that the original Adam was a composite being, from whom Eve was extracted. (A confirmation to Jewish scholars would be the change of number from singular to plural in Gen. 1.27.) The union is then clearly of a single man and a single woman.

Our Lord was, however, basing his prohibition of divorce not only on the words of the Torah which His Pharisee questioners were bound to accept, but also on the natural order established at Creation. This, as we saw in our second chapter, is the nearest thing that we have in our Lord's teaching to an appeal to Natural Law, and suggests that our Lord's standard is the proper standard for all men. Our Lord's authoritative pronouncement; "What therefore God has joined together, let not man put asunder," leaves no doubt that, for Christians at any rate, "No divorce" is the final word. W.

---

[8] Daube, *N.T. and Rabbinic Judaism*, pp. 71 ff.

Manson pointed out that Jesus here, in full consciousness of his authority as Messiah (recently exhibited in St Peter's confession, the Transfiguration, and the deliberate journey to Jerusalem), gave teaching about marriage, children, and the use of possessions. In regard to the two latter subjects, He made explicit reference to the Kingdom of God, and we may believe that with regard to marriage also He is revealing the law of the Kingdom. "Marriage is taken out of the old order regulated by statute and translated into the new order of Christ."[9] We have here clearly the law of Christ, but the modern question is whether we have any right to seek that this should be the standard accepted by the state in its laws. Our Lord's reference to what was in the beginning—the original order of Creation—goes some way towards giving us this right. Life-long monogamy is no limited ascetic vocation for a special group of Christians, like virginity or being made a eunuch for the Kingdom's sake; it is the natural way of marriage for mankind as such. We must admit that the positive law of the state, and indeed of the Church, should always take into account what is practicable, and that both these laws in different degree require to make concessions still to the hardness of men's hearts, but the standard of Christ to which we must bear witness in the rules of our Churches as well as in our preaching is the life-long union of one man and one woman.

§ 3

When we turn to the further teachings given by our Lord on this matter, we find differences in the various Gospels, difficulties in interpretation and doubtful texts. There is a corollary to the fundamental teaching, in which the consequence of divorce is said to be that one or more persons commit adultery. Mark represents Jesus as saying to the disciples privately "in the house"; "Whoever divorces his wife and marries another, commits adultery against her; and if she divorces her husband and marries another, she commits adultery" (Mk. x.11-12). Here the person who divorces his partner and remarries, without consideration of original guilt or innocence, is declared to be committing adultery. In Luke, where the fundamental

---

[9] C. of S. Report on Remarriage, 1957, p. 28.

teaching is not recorded, perhaps because the Genesis verses were thought to have no appeal to Gentile readers, our Lord also calls the husband who divorces his wife and marries again an adulterer, but adds that the new husband of the divorced woman is also committing adultery (Lk. xvi.18). In Matthew, in the Sermon on the Mount, our Lord again says that the new husband is committing adultery, and that the man divorcing his wife is driving her to adultery—a statement that was probably true to life at the time (Mt. v.31-2) In the Sermon on the Mount, however, there is no mention of the husband's own adultery; it may be that some Jewish Christian in passing on this teaching found it too violent a breach of Jewish tradition to suppose that a man exercising the universally recognised right of divorcing his wife was committing adultery. In Mt. xix. 9. however, we have the corollary just as it is in Mark and Luke; "Whoever divorces his wife . . . and marries another, commits adultery." This saying is so widely attested that we must accept it as a genuine saying of our Lord. The Church must still regard the man who institutes divorce proceedings with a view to a second marriage as about to commit adultery, even if circumstances be later found which modify this apparently harsh judgment.

About the genuineness of the other sayings about committing adultery through divorce, scholars are more hesitant. These may be, as Black suggests,[10] attempts to apply the original teachings of our Lord to the actual circumstances of the early Church, and it is possible that our present-day applications should be different. It may be that in parts of this teaching Jesus was condemning not the use but the abuse of the Mosaic law, by which innocent parties like a divorced wife and the man marrying a divorced woman, one who was not likely in Jewish custom to have been her lover, were made adulterers. One of the evils of our twentieth-century freedom to divorce is the way in which it puts innocent people into ambiguous situations, and the Church in its efforts to influence state legislation in this matter should have a special concern for such people.

In Mark alone there is reference to a woman divorcing her husband—a process unknown to Jewish law. There is,

[10] *C. of S. Report on Remarriage*, 1957, p. 22 f.

however, a Western reading which may be more primitive and which is in accord with Jewish practice; "If a woman *leaves* her husband and marries another, she commits adultery." The "leaving" here may mean the process of suing for divorce already mentioned, but in any case no law could prevent wilful desertion. The parallelism of the text as we have it suggests that it is an original Aramaic saying. The Sinaitic Syriac text actually puts the case of the woman leaving her husband first (an order that St Paul may have copied in 1 Cor. VII.10), and the strangeness of this order favours its originality. This order has been explained by the supposition that Jesus was referring to the case of Herodias, the notorious scandal of the time, and this would support Black's view that Jesus was condemning the abuse of the Mosaic law and not the law itself. It is likely that our Lord, contrary to Jewish tradition, was deliberately giving a woman and a man the same rights. This is the logical outcome of Jesus' teaching, however slow Christians have been in accepting it.

In the two relevant passages in Matthew (v.31-2, XIX.3-12), the prohibition of divorce is qualified by the words; "except on the ground of unchastity." This is commonly held to be a later addition to our Lord's teaching, possibly an accommodation to the teaching of the school of Shammai, which regarded unchastity as the only ground on which divorce was expedient, but even more probably a concession to human weakness. W. Manson pointed out that Mt. XIX.6, in spite of this exceptive clause, still gives our Lord's decisive word; "What . . . God has joined together, let no man put asunder." There also the exceptive clause, occurring as it does in reply to a new question about the Law of Moses, may refer only to the Mosaic rule, and not to the new law of Christ. Moses' real intention was that only the divorce of an unchaste wife should be allowed. Black also holds that the exceptive clause may have "a Dominical directive," but, even if this be so, we should, in my opinion, be unwise to use it to modify our Lord's fundamental teaching in view of our ignorance of the context in which the exception may originally have been made. Yet if the "no divorce" rule is to be modified because of the hardness of men's hearts, the exceptive clause gives us at least apostolic guidance as to the first exception to be made.

In Mt. xix an additional conversation with the disciples is recorded. Shocked either by this new idea of marriage as a life-long union or by our Lord's rescinding of the accepted Deuteronomic rule, they exclaim; "If such is the case . . . it is not expedient to marry." Our Lord's answer; "Not all men can receive this precept, but only those to whom it is given," may refer either to our Lord's own prohibition of divorce or to the disciples' statement as to the expediency of celibacy. If these words of Jesus, accepted by most scholars as authentic, did originally occur in this context and refer to the fundamental teaching, then we have Jesus admitting that His teaching on marriage cannot be received by all—a prediction that has unfortunately proved too true. This would leave the Mosaic permission for divorce available for those unable to accept Christ's higher standard. The ambiguity of the reference, however, makes it doubtful whether Jesus actually made such a concession. If He did, one wonders why the early Church held so strongly the view that marriage was a permanent union, and why St Paul had to give his own, and not the Lord's, opinion about mixed marriages.

§ 4

In 1 Cor. vii, St Paul, largely on his own authority, advocated a "stand-still" arrangement with regard to celibacy and marriage—a policy dictated by his expectation of an immediate Second Coming. In vss. 10 and 11 he states, on Christ's authority, (presumably the fundamental teaching and its corollary in Mk. x.11-12), that a wife should not leave her husband and that a husband should not divorce his wife. He adds that if a wife has left her husband, she should either remain unmarried or return. This latter appears to be St Paul's own advice, but it has our Lord's authority in His statement that such a wife on remarrying commits adultery. Nothing is said about the remarriage of a man who has divorced his wife; perhaps no such case had occurred in Corinth. What apparently had occurred were cases of a Christian husband divorcing a pagan wife, and St Paul, without authority from Christ, advises both against this and against a Christian wife divorcing her pagan husband. If the pagan partner insists on separation, then the Christian partner "is not bound." Most ancient commentators hold that this phrase means "is free to remarry," but several modern scholars deny this, holding that if St Paul had meant this, he would have said it explicitly (as he did in v. 39 of another situation), and that the whole tenor of the chapter is to discourage further marriage. Yet this does leave open the possibility that St Paul allowed certain Christians to marry again while their original partners were still alive, and the Roman Church still allows this "Pauline privilege" to converts from heathenism. It is very doubtful whether any party in a modern divorce case is in a position analogous to the Christian deserted by a pagan spouse. In no case does St Paul approve of a Christian taking the initiative in divorce proceedings, and this should still be the normal counsel given by a Christian minister. Those who say that our Lord's standards are unsuited for the conditions of the modern world should reflect that to St Paul they might have appeared even more unsuited to the conditions of licentious Corinth, but St Paul's witness remained clear.

The testimony of another Pauline passage (Eph. v.21-33) to the permanence of the marriage bond is more incidental. In the house-tables in Ephesians St Paul emphasises the wife's duty of submission and the husband's duty of love by using the analogy of Christ's love for the Church. As in our Lord's fundamental teaching, St Paul quotes Gen. II.24; "For this reason a man shall leave his father and mother and be joined to his wife, and the two shall become one." This quotation does imply that life-long monogamous marriage is part of the Divine order but this is not what St Paul is emphasising here. The word μυστήριον in vs. 32 refers primarily to Christ's relationship to the Church; marriage is not a mystery in the full New Testament meaning of the secret purpose of God now revealed in Jesus Christ. The sacramental view of marriage comes from St Paul having found in it a suitable symbol for the union of Christ and His Church.

§ 5

We shall make three comments on present discussions on this subject in the light of New Testament teaching.

First, the New Testament is far too realistic to hold that divorce is impossible, that to break the relationship of husband and wife is as impossible as to break the relationship of father and son. Even Romanists admit this in the case of the natural order of marriage when they allow converts the "Pauline privilege" of marrying again when their heathen partners are still alive.[11] The indissolubility view finds Scriptural basis chiefly in the "one flesh" of the Genesis quotation and in our Lord's words; "Whom God has joined together." A man, however, can, by his power of free choice, depart from God's ordinances; Adam could eat of the forbidden fruit, the Christian can deny the Baptism with which God has sealed him, and a man can separate from the wife to whom God has joined him. St Paul also uses the "one flesh" text in reference to a man's intercourse with a prostitute (1 Cor. vi.16), but no one would argue that this necessarily means that such a union is thereby indissoluble. What the New Testament teaches is that divorce is wrong, not that it is impossible, and it has no ecclesiastical sophistries about nullity, judicial separation, and the like.

Again, it is clear from the New Testament that difficulties were soon felt in the practical application of our Lord's standard in the rules of the Church, and such difficulties become greater when it is attempted to embody that standard in the law of a country. The Church's task today is to bear witness to this standard in face of very different standards of marriage. Opinions differ as to how this witness can be most effectively given, for example by disciplinary counsels to any Church member contemplating divorce or by the refusal to remarry any divorced person. The latter course is bound to mean great hardship for innocent people and truly penitent offenders, which Christian mercy must hesitate to impose. I should advocate it only because of the paramount need of a witness to Christ's standard in action as well as in word in this age of broken marriages.

Thirdly, our obsession with divorce and its problems may blind people today to the positive teaching of the New

[11] J. Lebreton, "La doctrine du renoncement dans le Nouveau Testament," henceforth cited as, "Renoncement dans le N.T," in *Nouvelle Revue théologique*, LXV (1938), p. 392: "Le péril créé par la foi brise le mariage."

Testament on marriage given chiefly in the house-tables (Eph. v.22-3; Col. iii.18-19; Tit. ii.3-8; 1 Pet. iii.1-7). Husbands are to love their wives, showing considerateness, honour, and lack of harshness. Wives are to submit to their husbands, and to be sensible, chaste, domestic, and kind. Without denying the permanent validity of these counsels if imaginatively applied, we must admit that the Christian outlook has moved towards regarding marriage as a more equal partnership, and for this the Christian ethic has been largely responsible. Today we do not regard the wife as in every way subject to her husband, just as we do not regard the employee as a slave bound to his master. The relationship of equal partnership in marriage is not only more Christian but also much more difficult practically than a relationship of domination and submission. The increased frequency of divorce since the general acceptance of the equal status of the sexes shows how much those entering marriage today need the grace of God to make the marriage what Christ wants it to be. The minister's part in a marriage is today a great evangelical opportunity for proclaiming to those about to be married that Gospel which alone contains the secret of the Christian love which is the sole guarantee of a permanent marriage in the modern world.

Literature

Report of the Special Committee of the General Assembly of the Church of Scotland on the Remarriage of Divorced Persons, Edinburgh 1957, esp. appendices I, II, and III by R. Yaron, M. Black, and W. Manson.

E. BRUNNER, *The Divine Imperative*, London 1937, chs. xxxi, xxxii.

W. LILLIE, *The Law of Christ*, London 1956, ch. v.

T. A. LACEY, *Marriage in Church and State*, revised by R. C. Mortimer, London 1947.

K. E. KIRK, *Marriage and Divorce*, 2nd edn. London 1948.

D. S. BAILEY, *The Mystery of Love and Marriage*, London 1952.

Chapter XII

The New Testament Attitude to Children

CHILDREN are part of the holy people of God, and are to be treated as such. If, as St Paul states (1 Cor. VII.14), the children of a marriage in which only one partner is a believer are by that fact holy, this is at least equally true of the children of two believing parents. Our Lord's declaration that the kingdom of God belongs to such children as those whom He took in His arms and blessed (Mk. x.14) implies that children can be truly members of His Church, and St Paul's inclusion of children in the house-tables in Colossians and Ephesians (Col. III.20-1; Eph. VI.1-4) indicates that children have within the Christian community duties and responsibilities suited to their position just like those of grown-up people in the various adult relationships of life. Children, of course, are different in many respects from grown-up people, and the New Testament accepts this as a plain fact; but their conduct, their worship, and their place in a Christian society are things to be taken seriously. To regard a children's service, and still more to plan it, as a kind of sacred entertainment, in which children "show off" their pious performances before their admiring parents and their cousins and their sisters and their aunts, partakes of blasphemy, and it does so because it does not regard the children as worshipping with simple sincerity the Father in spirit and in truth.

There is a difficulty here in the interpretation of New Testament language. Our Lord certainly on occasions addressed His disciples as "children" or even "little children," and referred to adult followers as "little ones who believe in me" (Mk. IX.42). St Paul and St John both address their readers in a similar fashion, for it was and still is the custom of an Eastern teacher to speak of his disciples as his children. A saying of our Lord, which in Mark clearly refers to the receiving of actual children (Mk. ix.37) refers in Matthew equally clearly to the receiving of grown-up disciples (Mt. x.40). The context of several of our Lord's sayings makes it clear that in them he has actual little children in mind, and it is perhaps more likely that a saying which originally referred to a child should come in apostolic tradition to refer to a disciple rather than the other way round. Be that as it may, even when Jesus spoke of adult disciples as children, He was not using this form of language either conventionally or sentimentally. Jesus addressed the disciples as children because, in regard to the matter about which He was talking, they either were or ought to be children. So we need have no hesitation in affirming that His words are, or should be, as true of children in age, as they were of the disciples of whom they may have been spoken. No one can doubt that our Lord condemns those who cause real children to stumble (Mk. ix.42) or approves of those who give them a cup of cold water in a time of need (Mt. x.42).

It is a fundamental error in interpretation to suppose that what Jesus emphasises in His teaching about little children is the moral example they provide. One wonders if Christian preachers who interpret the text; "To such belongs the kingdom of God" in terms of the innocence or loyalty or docility or humility or self-effacement of little children have ever heard of the doctrine of Original Sin, or have ever faced at close quarters a class of actual children. Every teacher knows that even very small children are, just like grown-up people, a very mixed bunch as regards their moral qualities, and Jesus Himself had noticed how quarrelsome and uncooperative children can be while playing games in the street (Mt. xi.16, 17). The real objection, however, to such moralising interpretations is that they make little children enter the Kingdom of God on the basis of works or merit, and that would be a complete overturning of the whole Christian Gospel.

There is certainly one saying in which Jesus appears at first sight to be attributing to little children the moral quality of humble-mindedness; "Whoever humbles himself like this child, he is the greatest in the kingdom of heaven" (Mt. xviii.4). Self-abasement is by no means a characteristic practice of small children, and this fact should make us look at the saying more closely. The Greek root ταπεινός, found in the verb here, has, like its English equivalent "humble," both moral and non-moral usages. English people used to talk of a person as being of humble birth without any intention to disparage the person's parents or circumstances, still less to suggest that there was any virtue in them; they were simply pointing to a fact in the structure of society. In Greek literature generally, and particularly in the New Testament, when the word ταπεινός is used without any qualification (such as "lowly *in heart*" (Mt. xi.29)), it often means "humble" in this non-moral factual sense. The one possible exception in the New Testament is in ii Cor. x.1, where St Paul describes himself as ταπεινός when face to face with the Corinthians, but even here St Paul may be referring to the social status assigned to him by the Corinthians. The New Testament has a compound noun ταπεινοφροσύνη meaning humble-mindedness with a definitely moral significance, but this word is never used directly of children. What ταπεινός and the verb from it indicate in the New Testament is the objective state of a person, his low birth, his poor circumstances, his state of weakness, despondency or subordination, perhaps even his diffidence of manner, but not a moral quality. The normal opposite to "the humble" is "the exalted," not "the proud." Even the quotation from Proverbs used both in i Peter and James; "God opposes the proud, but gives grace to the humble" (Prov. iii.34; i Pet. v.5; Jas. iv.6) probably referred in the original to well-known classes in the community, the "haves" and the "have-nots" rather than to their moral qualities. Of course "humble-mindedness" is a fitting quality for children because their status is one of subordination.

What follows from all this is that the man "who humbles himself like this child" is assuming the status and not the moral qualities of the child. He comes to Jesus not offering his humility or his innocency, but just as he is described in a well-known hymn; "Nothing in my hands I bring." There is an interesting parallelism in language between the Synoptic saying; "Unless you turn and become like children, you will never enter the kingdom of heaven" (Mt. xviii.3), and the Johannine saying; "Unless one is born anew, he cannot see

the kingdom of God" (Jn. III.3). The reason why the condition of entering the kingdom is the assumption of the status
of a child, is that this is the state nearest to that of the unborn
child, one which Nicodemus and the rest of us think it impossible
to reach. The child is the pattern of the entrant into the
kingdom because, having nothing in himself, he has to receive
everything from Christ.

Paradoxically, all this teaching reveals the importance of
children, something, as a headmistress recently remarked,
that the children themselves should not know but that grown-up
people should know. We have here in our Lord's teaching a
complete reversal of ordinary worldly standards. Children,
who were so unimportant in the ancient world, so numerous,
and often so short-lived, are among the last who shall be first.
"From our human point of view, the wise and understanding,
the great ones of the earth, the mature adults, are the most
suitable candidates for Baptism: in Jesus' way of thinking the
most suitable are the babes, the little ones who trust in Him,
the infants in whose way no one dare set a stumbling-block—
those, in fact, who can most readily begin again."[1]

§ 2

There is a double relationship between childhood and manhood. The adult, as we have just seen, needs to turn and
become as a little child, and so there should be always something of the child in the mature Christian. On the other hand
the child needs to grow into a man "in wisdom and in stature
and in favour with God and man," as Luke (II.52) summed up
the natural development of the child Jesus. St Paul obviously
had little use for Christians who remain at the stage of needing
their mother's milk and who display the quarrelsomeness of
undisciplined children (I Cor. III.1-3). We are to be "no
longer children tossed to and fro and carried about with every
wind of doctrine" (Eph. IV.14). It is in evil only that we
should be babes, but we should be mature in our Christian
thinking (I Cor. XIV.20). It is still one of the problems of the
educator to deal with children in such a way that they grow
out of those childish qualities with which St Paul found fault

[1] Church of Scotland, *The Biblical Doctrine of Baptism*, Edinburgh 1958, p. 52.

in his converts, and yet keep the status of childhood which qualifies them for entrance into the kingdom.

The method of remaining one of Christ's little ones while growing up into Christian manhood is the way of obedience. "Children, obey your parents in the Lord, for this is right" (Eph. VI.1). "Children, obey your parents in everything, for this pleases the Lord" (Col. III.20). The special duty of the child is to obey, not to think for himself; "by obeying one learns how to obey,"[2] and this is the first step in learning how to make decisions for oneself, for which the child must have increasing opportunities as he grows older. St Paul appears wholeheartedly to be in agreement with the Wisdom literature of the Old Testament on the importance of obedience for children. In this children have the example of Jesus Himself, who according to Luke (II.51) was obedient to His parents in Nazareth, and who, according to Hebrews (v.8) "learned obedience through what He suffered." The Church today tends to neglect in its teaching the duty of obedience; she is afraid of losing her hold on young people, and tries, as Bonhoeffer remarks, "to keep up with the young" in their disregard of their elders.[3] The New Testament certainly gives no support to theories of uncontrolled self-expression based on some pseudo-psychology or to practices of disobedience formed because of the sloth and self-indulgence of parents. The child who is allowed with impunity to disobey his parents is being deprived of an essential part of life's training, for the child who does not obey the earthly father whom he has seen, is very unlikely to learn to obey the heavenly Father whom he has not seen.

It is unfair and unwise to give great weight to this instruction to children in the house-tables, as parents of a past generation used to do, without giving equal weight to the corresponding instruction to parents. "Fathers, do not provoke your children, lest they become discouraged" (Col. III.21). "Fathers, do not provoke your children to anger" (Eph. VI.4). The provoking of children may result in their anger (according to most manuscripts of Ephesians) or in their discouragement (according to Colossians). This twofold consequence suggests two

---

[2] C. S. Lewis, *George Macdonald, an Anthology*, p. 118.
[3] Bonhoeffer, *Ethics*, p. 49.

different kinds of provocation. There is the playful teasing of children with the more or less deliberate intention of provoking them to anger for the entertainment of the teaser, and sometimes with the expressed excuse that this is good training for the child. It is hard to believe that such adults would regard teasing by other people as a good discipline for their grown-up selves, and the rough places of life provide sufficient natural causes of provocation without artificial ones being added by stupid people in search of entertainment. There is, on the other hand, the discouragement that comes to children from an over-multiplication of commands requiring obedience. It sometimes appears as if grown-up people, and particularly the older sisters of small brothers, try to provide for little children a code of rules more detailed than that which the Pharisees and their successors deduced from the Law of Moses; and the youngsters, finding such a code impossible to obey, lose heart. The guiding principle in the matter, which is suggested by this teaching and by modern educational theory, is to give children as few orders as possible but to see that they are obeyed without question. Of course if the purpose of an order can be explained to a child so much the better for his training in self-discipline, but it is not always possible or even desirable for a child to understand why a parent tells him to do something, and the child should learn that his parent's bidding is sufficient reason for obedience. If more of our own generation had learned this obedience as children, they might now be more ready, as men and women, to obey the Word of God without question. There are of course other ways, as well as obedience to instructions, through which children learn what they need to learn, such as suggestion, co-operation in play, or even the experience of "burning their fingers." So we should give a child a good deal of freedom, even freedom to be a little naughty, but in what is really important we should demand unquestioning obedience. Even preachers and lecturers on Christian ethics might do well to use this same method in dealing with the grown-up "children" to whom they speak in apostolic fashion. Let us be as clear and bold as we can about God's command when that command is given unambiguously in Scripture; elsewhere let us leave moral issues to the judgment and decision of our hearers.

In this connexion both our Lord and St Paul refer to the Fifth Commandment, and it is significant that St Paul, even in his later teaching to Gentiles, still regards this commandment as binding on Christians, and as holding a promise for them. The Hebrew word translated "honour" here implies not only an attitude of respect for those in authority but also the obedience of which we have spoken and the caring for parents in their old age. Although we know little of the custom of declaring property "Corban," it was clearly regarded by our Lord as a shameful way of evading the plain moral duty of supporting one's parents (Mk. vii.11-13), and in the Pastoral Epistles too it is said to be a religious duty to make some return to one's parents, especially to a widowed mother (1 Tim. v.4). The provision made by the Welfare State has made no fundamental difference to this obligation; what old people need is friendship, consideration, and personal interest, more than money. The Fifth Commandment is not set aside by St Paul's statement elsewhere that "children ought not to lay up for their parents, but parents for their children" (ii Cor. xii.14). St Paul is here defending his own position as a father-in-God with ironic humour, and it is a little far-fetched to suppose that he is referring to the bad custom in the ancient world of treating children as economic assets.[4] Yet even this counsel is a reminder that in Christ all these obligations are mutual; parents must do their best for their children and children for their parents. In speaking of the Fifth Commandment, St Paul refers to the attached promise; "that it may be well with you and that you may live long on the earth" (Eph. vi.3). This was originally in all probability a promise of a lasting settlement in the land of Palestine. The Shorter Catechism interpretation, which suggests a promise of long life and prosperity to the individual,[5] is scarcely confirmed by experience, even with the qualification the Catechism makes. The society in which children learn to obey their parents in their homes, and so learn both to discipline themselves and to submit to the necessary laws of their community, is likely to be a more permanent society than that in which the mutual obligations of the home are neglected. "Here the child learns," says Brunner ". . . to know in an

---

[4] Marshall, *N.T. Ethics*, p. 339 f.
[5] *Shorter Catechism*, Answer 66.

K

exemplary way the fundamental relation of community, the sense of connexion through the mutual need of one another. . . . What the child learns in this intercourse with his father and his mother, is far more important than anything that he can learn in school. . . . The essential thing in the family is not a material or spiritual something but the actual fact of community."[6] It is this lesson learned through obedience that helps to establish a permanent society.

The two words translated "discipline" and "instruction," used by St Paul in his counsel to fathers, refer to two distinct aspects of education.[7] This is obscured in the familiar Authorised Version translation: "the nurture and admonition of the Lord" (Eph. VI.4). The Greek παιδεία does not mean "nurture" in the New Testament, whatever it may have meant in Classical Greek; it refers to the sterner method of education, correction by punishment. In Hebrews XII.6, where the discipline of children is used as an illustration of God's discipline of His people, we are told that the Lord "chastises every son whom he receives"; "chastise" is the word used in the Gospel of our Lord being scourged in the court of Pilate. There can be little doubt that both in Ephesians and in Hebrews corporal punishment is regarded as a normal part of παιδεία. The theological justification for sternness in the discipline of children—a sternness that may or may not involve corporal punishment—is that God is stern in the discipline of His older children when they need it. God does not always deal gently with His people, as Job and the Psalmists knew, and as all experience confirms. If God had wanted this universe to be a place for indulging human beings in the way that many modern parents indulge their children, He should have made it very differently. In his last letter to his wife, written before his death in the Antarctic, Captain Scott wrote about the upbringing of his son; "Make him a strenuous man."[8] That is God's way of bringing up His children, and we can have no better example.

To deal with St Paul's other term, "instruction" or νουθεσία

---

[6] Brunner, *Divine Imperative*, p. 512.

[7] A. Monod, *Explication de l'épître de Saint Paul aux Éphésiens*, Paris 1867, p. 407; "Ce sont les deux grands moyens de l'éducation; l'un sévère, l'autre doux: corriger, pour reprimer le péché, et enseigner, pour le prévenir."

[8] R. F. Scott, *Scott's Last Expedition*, one vol. edn., London 1923, p. 475.

would raise the whole question of Christian education, which is much too large a theme for this chapter. We must, however, refer to one clear indication in the New Testament. Two passages in II Timothy (1.5, III.14-17), which I cannot but regard as genuine writings of St Paul, make it clear that in the education of Timothy the Holy Scriptures played a central part. The picture of the child Timothy instructed in the Scriptures by mother and grandmother is a model for Christian education. The work of teacher and minister is here secondary, however richly it may be used. The primary influence is that of the parents, especially of the mother, and there can be no Christian education equal to that which she gives. The godless conditions of the modern world have demanded substitutes for this in the form of day schools, Sunday schools, and youth organisations, but we must never lose sight of the fact that these are substitutes, *Ersätze*, for the Christian education of the home. As for the school itself, may not one of the chief reasons for our failure in saving children from delinquency be the subordinate place to which the teaching of the Bible has been relegated in most schools?

§ 3

Our Lord had apparently more to say about the danger of family obligations coming in the way of one's Christian duty than about these obligations themselves. Jesus Himself did recognise such obligations, possibly by working as a carpenter in Nazareth (Mk. VI.3) and so supporting His mother and her children, and certainly by committing His mother to the care of the beloved disciple when He was on the Cross (Jn. XIX.25-7). Yet these obligations took a second place to His Father's will and work. As soon as He became a son of the Law, He showed a certain independence of His parents by remaining in the Temple for instruction (Lk. II.41-8), and later, during His ministry, when He was sought out by His mother and brothers, He deliberately refused to do what they wanted—presumably return home (Mk. III.21, 31-4). Jesus saw that one inevitable consequence of His mission was to be the breaking-up of families (Mt. x.35), although this need not have been His deliberate intention, as some English translations suggest. A man may have to act as if he hated his own family (Lk. XIV.26);

"hate" in Semitic idiom does not always imply actual hostility, but can indicate, as here, that love of family must take second place to the love of Christ. Jesus' refusal to allow a would-be disciple to bury his father (Lk. ix.59-60) seems to us unduly harsh and inconsiderate, but it is probable that the man was putting off his decision to follow Christ for an indefinite period until his father might die, and the danger of such postponement is obvious. Or it may be that in this particular case, Jesus saw that even an hour or two's delay in order to make the funeral arrangements would divert this man from his purpose. Not even the most sacred family obligation must come in the way of allegiance to Christ.

What Jesus saw, and what modern Communists have also seen, is the danger of family obligations becoming an excuse for selfishness and lack of public spirit. Parents determined to do the best for their children may show great self-denial, considerateness, and other Christian virtues for the sake of the one or two children in their home without realising that through these same virtues they are teaching their children a disregard for the claims of others and a narrow selfishness that can only lead to spiritual disaster. Even mother-love— that paragon of the virtues in the sentimental humanism of today—apart from the love of God in Christ, may be only "comparable to a cat's love for her kittens or a sow's devotion to her litter."[9] We shall see in a later study that one of the problems for Christian ethics to consider today is how this natural family affection may be transformed into the love that Jesus came to pour out into men's hearts.

An auxiliary way of combating the narrow exclusiveness of the family is to recognise that obedience to parents is primarily important as a way of learning obedience to God. In modern schools children learn arithmetic by working out certain practical problems relevant to their own limited conditions, like dealings in the tuck-shop or measurements for their handwork. No one, however, supposes that they are learning arithmetic for these schoolboy purposes; they are learning arithmetic so that they may conduct efficiently the business of adult life. It is the same to a large extent with obedience to parents; it is not to be regarded merely as a

[9] Marshall, *N.T. Ethics*, p. 141.

means to secure some order in the home, necessary as that may be, but as a training in obedience to God. And when the young person is emancipated from the tutelage of parents and teachers, he should remember two things. Just as in school we are being trained for adult life in this world, so the whole of our human life is a preparation for the life of eternity. He should remember also that Christ's demand to us as grown-up people is that we should turn again and become as little children. This paradoxical element in the Christian life is integral to the conception of self-denial which we shall study in a later chapter.

Literature

E. BRUNNER, *The Divine Imperative*, London 1937, pp. 367-373, 504-16.
L. H. MARSHALL, *The Challenge of New Testament Ethics*, London 1948, pp. 136-42, 339-40.
CHURCH OF SCOTLAND, *The Biblical Doctrine of Baptism*, Edinburgh 1958, pp. 45-54.

Chapter XIII

Eschatology and Ethics in the New Testament

CERTAIN views that have been held in the past as to the relevance of Christian eschatology for ethics are out of fashion today; most conspicuously the preaching of hell-fire as a sanction for ensuring good conduct has almost disappeared from our pulpits. Yet it is worth while to try to discover the measure of truth in such views from the New Testament itself. This consideration is made difficult today by the variety of eschatologies taught by New Testament scholars, although there seems to be increasing agreement about two basic positions. The New Age, the last times, or the time of the Kingdom of God began in the life, death, and resurrection of Jesus Christ; this truth is over-emphasised in C. H. Dodd's "realised eschatology." On the other hand the Kingdom of God will not be manifested in its full power until the "end" which is pictured in the various New Testament symbols of the Second Coming, the Last Judgment, and the new heaven and the new earth; this is the truth that is over-emphasised in the "futurist eschatology" of many conservative theologians.

The view which is most out of fashion among theologians today, although it is still held vaguely by many Christians and, more strangely, by many people outside the Church, may be called "progressive eschatology." It holds that the Kingdom began with the mission of Jesus and is growing, either in a steady progress or in successive waves of advance and retreat, until it will reach a final consummation, which the more pious identify with Christ's coming in glory according to the Scriptures. Biblical support for this view was found in the parables of gradual growth (particularly that of the mustard seed), which are now commonly interpreted with a different emphasis, and in the petition "Thy kingdom come" in the

Lord's prayer. It is a view clearly expressed in many missionary hymns and it was basic to the "social gospel" which was prevalent, especially in America, during the earlier part of this century. This gospel emphasised the social message of the prophets and the ethical teaching of Jesus with a this-worldly view of the Kingdom of God. Christian ethics seemed more important than Christian theology, for the task of Christians was to work for the establishment of the Kingdom, or, in St Paul's phraseology (Col. IV.11), to be "fellow workers for the kingdom of God." The challenge of this Gospel is given in a very popular hymn,

> Rise up, O men of God !
> The Church for you doth wait,
> Her strength unequal to her task,
> Rise up and make her great.

Most theologians today have, under the influence of Barth, rejected this view. The Kingdom of God, they point out, according to the New Testament, comes down from God out of heaven (Rev. XXI.2), and is the product of God's grace and not of human endeavour. "Thy kingdom come" is a prayer addressed to God and not to ourselves.

What is wrong with this view is that it regards the consummation as merely the result of a progressive development largely brought about by human effort. But our realisation of the limitations and distortions of this "progressive eschatology" must not blind us to what the New Testament says in its support. While Jesus appears to have given first place in His teaching to the more apocalyptic view of the Kingdom associated with the mysterious title "Son of man," he never rejected that Messianic hope of the prophets for this world in which social and economic factors played a part, and even "back of the visions and rhapsodies of the apocalyptists lay social dreams and urges, wants and aspirations."[1] Jesus called disciples to share in His work, which included the healing of bodies as well as the preaching of the Gospel. What St Paul says about individual salvation is also relevant in work for the kingdom; "Work out your own salvation with fear and trembling; for God is at work in

[1] F. C. Grant, "Ethics and eschatology in the teaching of Jesus," in *Journal of Religion*, XXII (1942), pp. 360 ff.

you" (Phil. II.12-13). Human effort is the necessary response to Divine grace, however secondary its place may be in the Gospel. We find echoes in the Gospel of a Jewish view that the time of the Messiah could be hastened by the performance of good works and particularly by repentance. Rabbi Levi (c. A.D. 300) wrote; "If all Israel together would only repent for a single day, the redemption would be vouchsafed almost immediately."[2] Such a view may lie behind the announcement of both John the Baptist and Jesus Himself; "Repent, for the kingdom of heaven is at hand" (Mt. III.2; IV.17). This repentance was, of course, religious as well as moral; it is a turning to God even more than a turning away from evil, but it certainly includes moral elements as John the Baptist made clear in the practical advice he gave to different enquirers. A similar Jewish belief may lie behind a Christian view that the Second Coming is delayed until the number of the elect is made up. Our Lord declared that before the final consummation "the Gospel must be first preached to all nations" (Mk. XIII.10). It almost looks as if the full realisation of the Kingdom may depend on individual human decisions in this matter of repentance. Common sense would at least maintain that each individual who rejects the call of Christ is shutting himself out of the Kingdom and to that limited extent at least is hindering the fullness of its coming.

Our Lord's saying that the Gospel must be first preached to all nations indicates that one part which Christians have in the establishment of the Kingdom is that of witnessing to Christ. Work, as we have already seen,[3] is in the New Testament very commonly the work of bearing a Christian witness in the world. Such work has often a definitely eschatological setting in the New Testament. St Paul, in the light of his great discourse on the resurrection of the dead, exhorts his readers; "Therefore, my beloved brethren, be steadfast, immovable, always abounding in the *work* of the Lord, knowing that in the Lord your *labour* is not in vain" (1 Cor. xv.58). There is a similar indication in the statement in Rev. XIV.13 that those who die in the Lord are blessed because "their deeds follow

---

[2] Quoted A. N. Wilder, *Eschatology and Ethics in the Teaching of Jesus*, henceforth cited as *Eschatology and Ethics*, revised edn., New York 1950, p. 83.
[3] See Chapter x.

them." While the Kingdom is essentially God's Kingdom, which He alone can bring to its consummation, we too have a part in it, and we do need today to realise the ultimate importance of our Christian endeavours. The rejection of the "social gospel" in a too humanistic form has left many Christian thinkers with the feeling that good works accomplish nothing and indeed dangerously stimulate human pride. The New Testament, however, makes it clear that our endeavours have a place, not merely in alleviating the sufferings and deprivations of the present order, but also in the accomplishing of God's ultimate plan for His Kingdom.

§ 2

Another view that is somewhat lightly rejected today is the view of Weiss and Schweitzer that much of the ethical teaching of Jesus was an *Interimsethik*, which was intended only for the short time between His own day and the expected coming of the Kingdom. It was an ethic given to meet a special emergency, not to meet the continued needs of the life of the world. It is easy to point out a number of misconceptions in this theory of an interim ethic. (*a*) While much of Jesus' moral teaching has an eschatological background, as in the references to the Kingdom of heaven in the Beatitudes (Mt. v.3-12), that teaching does not commonly use the language of the contemporary apocalypses. It uses more frequently the kind of language that we find in the Wisdom literature of the Old Testament and the Apocrypha; there are many such echoes of Wisdom literature in the Sermon on the Mount. But even the use of apocalyptic language does not mean that Jesus either Himself accepted or wished His hearers to accept all current apocalyptic views. (The parable of Dives and Lazarus (Lk. xvi.19-31) is a good example of Jesus' using a contemporary picture of the life beyond death in order to bring home a religious truth without His necessarily accepting the literal truth of the picture.) St Paul, in similar fashion, used Stoic ways of speech, particularly in his ethical teaching, but he certainly did not accept the Stoic philosophy. (*b*) The "interim ethic" theory has beome linked with the view that the moral teaching of Jesus is impracticable—impossible for ordinary people to carry out in their common lives. It could only be practised, this view suggests, by people in a high state of tension expecting the immediate return of their Lord. While the Sermon on the Mount, which is the part of our Lord's teaching most commonly described as impractical, is profoundly eschatological, it makes no direct reference to the immediacy of the *parousia,* and much of it is obviously teaching for a settled community rather than for an excited group facing an immediate end of the present order. It has to do with such permanent moral problems as unsettled quarrels, ostentatious religious practices, and worry about food and clothing. (c) Both our Lord and St Paul teach that the best way of preparing for the strange, apocalyptic events that appear imminent, is the faithful carrying out of one's common duties, not the adoption of an emergency ethic. The servant to be commended at his Lord's coming is the one who carries on watchfully with his ordinary business. St Paul uses very plain language to bring this home to his Thessalonian readers, culminating in the maxim; "If any one will not work, let him not eat" (ii Thess. iii.6-13). (d) The view that "only things which would survive the passing of heaven and earth were worthy of attention,"[4] which naturally accompanied the expectation of an immediate end to the present order, had a very mixed moral influence on those holding it. On the Thessalonians its influence appears to have been definitely bad, and perhaps even St Paul himself was hindered at one period of his life from a fully Christian view of marriage and the family by his expectation of an immediate *parousia.*

There is a fundamental truth, however, in the "interim ethic" theory which its critics sometimes fail to see. We in the twentieth century are still living in the interim period, the period after the Kingdom has come in Christ but before the Kingdom has come in its final power and glory. It is a period in which, as St Paul saw, we are engaged in a struggle against cosmic powers of evil. "For we are not contending against flesh and blood, but against principalities, against the powers, against the world rulers of this present darkness, against the spiritual hosts of wickedness in the heavenly places" (Eph. vi.12). Preachers commonly interpret this text in terms of the

---

[4] Dodd, *Gospel and Law,* p. 28.

individual's continued struggle against temptation, but St Paul's language here and elsewhere suggests a larger struggle against organised spiritual forces of evil, and it was thus that Revelation saw the Roman Empire and its Caesar-worship. It is true that Christ won the decisive battle against these powers in His death and resurrection, but in the interim period these powers, though doomed, are only too evidently active in this world, and the Christian life is properly regarded as a warfare against them. Nazism, Fascism, scientific materialism, and atheistic Communism are either such spiritual powers or their manifestations active in our own time. There are those who think that the Christian's part in such warfare is confined to the preaching of the Gospel to the world, praying for the world, and giving in the life of the Church an example for society to follow. These were in New Testament times the only world-directed activities in which Christians could engage as minority communities in countries occupied by Rome, and they are still the characteristic activities of Christian minorities in heathen countries. The Church has in more or less "Christian countries" to play the prophet's part of watchman, warning Caesar when he is exceeding his powers and calling the nation to a repentance that may even demand revolt.[5] In combating the forces of evil, Christians will even use political means if these are available. "Those sincerely engaged in a total war do not confine themselves to the conventional weapons used by their ancestors in very different circumstances," and one part of the Christian watchfulness which our Lord enjoined should be to watch for every opportunity, however secular, of striking a blow against the powers of evil.

All would agree that the Christian's primary duty in this interim period is to bear witness by word and deed to what Christ has done. This witness obviously could not be given by ordinary people before Christ came; even the prophets who did bear a witness to the Coming One could only do so in a very different way from that in which the simplest Christian can now give his testimony. After the interim period there

---

[5] A. N. Wilder, "Kerygma, eschatology and social ethics," in *The Background of the New Testament and its Eschatology*, edd. W. D. Davies and D. Daube, Cambridge 1956, p. 515, cf. Ezek. XXXIII.

will be no need of witness, "For they shall all know me from the least of them to the greatest" (Jer. xxxi.34). A. N. Wilder, who rejects the theory of an "interim ethic" in its original form, still maintains that special demands are "made upon the disciples in the short period when the Kingdom is still struggling with the present evil age." He draws a parallel between the ethical demands of the apostolic age and those of the modern mission field. "If one thinks of the practical issues of a mission field in our own day one can easily recognise two types of occasion for extraordinary and exacting demands. In the first place, the converts—especially those with ten talents, or indicated by their freedom from various handicaps and responsibilities—will be called upon for extraordinary effort and devotion in view of the greatness of the opportunity and the fewness of the laborers. In the second place, over against the old life and its ethics which may be exerting a strong pull upon those that are leaving it, a sharp demand may well be laid upon the vacillating disciples bidding them endure the persecutions and costly renunciations incident to their reformation, and pointing out the inescapable moral issues and the penalties involved. Such a twofold aspect we see in the sterner sayings of Jesus, some addressed to disciples calling them to the uniquely great occasion and opportunity and responsibility of the mission; some bringing home to the more general type of hearer the sacrifices he must be prepared to make and the cleavages he must be ready to accept in espousing the gospel."[6] The situation which is so truly described here is not confined to the apostolic age and the modern mission field; it is the situation in which every Christian finds himself in the period "between the times"; it is certainly the situation in which every Christian with any insight finds himself in Britain today.

In the interim period the Christian is at the same time living both in the old age and in the new. He may do his daily work at Philippi but his citizenship is in heaven; he may live at Corinth, but he is also in Christ. This, as we have already said, is the cause of a certain detachment in the attitude of Christians to the problems of politics and economics—something which the zealous moral reformer finds inopportune and incomprehensible. In the light of what is unseen and

---

[6] Wilder, *Eschatology and Ethics*, p. 190 f.

eternal the Christian sees the relativity and partiality of human schemes of reform. This fact of the two ages may explain the alternation in the New Testament between concrete moral counsels and a doctrine of grace which takes the Christian beyond good and evil. It may be that our ambiguous position is better expressed in the language of Jewish apocalyptic than that of modern theology.

§ 3

A third view, commonly neglected today, is the relevance of a final judgment to morality. The New Testament has no doubt of the reality of such a judgment. It appears in many parables, including that of the sheep and goats, where the criterion of judgment is explicitly ethical. It appears in straightforward statements like St Paul's declaration; "For we must all appear before the judgment seat of Christ, so that each one may receive good or evil, according to what he has done in the body" (II Cor. v.10), or our Lord's warning; "The Son of man . . . will repay every man for what he has done" (Mt. xvi.27). In Revelation we have apocalyptic pictures of the great white throne, of city gates closed to evil-doers, and of a lake burning with fire and brimstone.

Many set all this aside as part of an outmoded Jewish apocalyptic. Paul Ramsey writes; "Few contemporary Christians accept the kind of kingdom-expectation Jesus considered of central importance, and rightly they do not."[7] He then points out that Jesus' expectation that "the *living* God would soon, suddenly and catastrophically put an end to the present age" is supported neither by the theories of the scientists nor by the historical crises of our time. We reply that it is the business of the preacher and of the teacher of New Testament ethics to present the Gospel truth that remains after the apocalyptic language of the first century is discarded, and to present it in the light of modern scientific theories of the running down of the universe and of the self-destructive power man has taken to himself in the mid-twentieth century. The outcome will assuredly be that it is as easy for us as it was for the Christians of the first century to believe in God's word of judgment.

[7] P. Ramsey, *Basic Christian Ethics*, London 1953, p. 35 f.

A more cogent objection to accepting the doctrine of the Last Judgment is that it appears to imply in a glorified eschatological form a prudential commercial morality which finds its justifications in rewards and its sanctions in punishments. Even in those parts of Jesus' teaching where the apocalyptic language is not evident, there is a good deal of emphasis on rewards and punishments; those who seek the praise of men for their pious practices have already had all the reward they deserve, but the reward of the truly pious is great in heaven. Our Lord's language in such passages may be influenced by the prudential maxims of the Wisdom literature and of the Jewish Rabbis. Yet the notion of a final judgment is far too explicit and widespread throughout the whole New Testament to be explained away as a mere concession to contemporary forms of thought or language. It is a fundamental part of the apostolic *kerygma* as of later creeds.

There are certain considerations which may help us to appreciate the teaching of a final judgment as an incentive to good conduct.

1. The doctrine of a last judgment brings home to us the gravity of moral choices. Our choices of right or wrong are no mere short-term policies without any permanent significance; still less are they meaningless illusions, as the Hindu philosophers often suggest; they are important factors in the ultimate destiny of ourselves and of the universe. Jacques Ellul finds the terrible seriousness of human law in the fact that God makes use of it as part of the criteria of His judgment.[8] We Christians can remain quite unperturbed at naturalistic theories of the origin of our moral judgments in human emotions and the like; it is not from their origin that they derive their validity; it is from the fact that God makes use of them in His judgment. In apocalyptic language what is important and final tends to be depicted as near and imminent; the judgment is to come on this generation (Mk. XIII.30); those standing here will see the Kingdom of God come with power (Mk. IX.1). There is a truth of common sense in this language, for, as the historian Ranke said, every generation is at the same distance from eternity. We need not imagine, as St Paul's Thessalonian readers did (I Thess. IV.15), that those alive at the time of the

[8] Ellul, *Theological Foundation*, p. 95.

parousia are especially fortunate, or that, on the contrary, they alone face judgment. A great deal of the loose thinking about evolution today makes a similar mistake; the later generations in history are considered more fortunate merely because they come later. Biblical writers may have been wrong in their expectation that the *parousia* events would take place in their own generation, but they were absolutely right in holding that the martyrs of the first century had as direct an access to the heavenly city as those who will be alive when Christ comes again. Apocalyptic literature sees eternity breaking into time, and this inevitably means the judgment of men's actions *sub specie aeternitatis*. We see this in the eschatological event that has already taken place in the incarnation of our Lord. "Thou judgest us: Thy purity doth all our lusts condemn," is the way that this is expressed in a familiar hymn, and no man can face God incarnate as He is revealed to us in the Gospels without an automatic judgment taking place on his own sinful desires. This will be even more true when we see Him face to face.

2. We are perhaps a little vain when we imagine that we can do without the hope of reward or the fear of punishment. Of course we should all seek goodness for goodness' sake or, better still, for the glory of God, but do we not all need a little encouragement in doing what is right—at least some evidence that virtue is its own reward? The heaven of Moslem literalists with its merely sensual pleasures is certainly not the kind of reward that Christians should desire; but a heaven, the very essence of which is to be with Christ, is a reward that Christians ought to long for and work for. A well-done action is in a very real way its own reward, and the joy of heaven may consist largely in such accomplishings. Our Lord at any rate had no scruples about encouraging His disciples in ways of good by the assurance that their rewards were great in heaven. There is a practical realism in this teaching which takes us as we are. I am sometimes a little amused at those modern schools where there are supposedly no rewards or punishments; I confess to the suspicion that the children in them are often punished by more wounding techniques than the use of the tawse, and are often rewarded by more subtly pleasing satisfactions than the dull tomes which used to be given as prizes. There is no

exaggeration of the place of rewards in the Bible; good actions are normally done not "to secure the mercy [of God], but in gratitude for it."[9]

3. The eschatological teaching of the New Testament bears witness to the fundamental righteousness that is at the heart of the universe. However honestly men have held that goodness is to be sought for goodness' sake, they have never been content to believe that the good will always suffer, and that the wicked will prosper permanently. We may make the same mistake as some Old Testament writers did and think that the outcome of goodness should necessarily be material prosperity—"health, wealth, and happiness" in our modern speech; the outcome of goodness is something more spiritual, more transcendent, more eternal. The Bible teaches that when the whole story of the universe is viewed from the angle of eternity, moral evil and ultimate destruction are inseparably bound together, and we may have glimpses of this in Biblical apocalypses or in hard facts of history. Equally moral goodness and man's ultimate welfare are inseparably linked, for the Bible conception of judgment always includes the vindication of goodness. C. H. Dodd maintains that the final event "would bring upon men at once judgment and salvation, judgment absolute and salvation absolute, and would reveal the Kingdom of God, that is to say, the sovereignty of God over His world."[10] If there were not such a final judgment, the story of this universe could only be

> "a tale
> Told by an idiot, full of sound and fury,
> Signifying nothing."

Literature

A. N. WILDER, *Eschatology and Ethics in the Teaching of Jesus*, revised edition, New York 1950.

A. N. WILDER, "Kerygma, eschatology and social ethics," in *The Background of the New Testament and its Eschatology*, edd. W. D. Davies and D. Daube, Cambridge 1956.

O. CULLMANN, *Christ and Time*, London 1951. Translation of *Christus und die Zeit*, Zurich 1946.

---

[9] Wilder, *Eschatology and Ethics*, p. 93.
[10] Dodd, *Gospel and Law*, p. 27.

Chapter XIV

The Christian Conception of Self-denial

THE last phrase of the commandment; "You shall love your neighbour *as yourself*" seems scarcely consistent with the repeated saying of our Lord; "If any man would come after me, *let him deny himself*" (Mk. VIII.34; Mt. X.38, XVI.24; Lk. IX.23, XIV.27; cf. Jn. XII.25). It is a common fact of human experience that men naturally love themselves and wish their own good; St Paul says; "No man ever hates his own flesh, but nourishes and cherishes it" (Eph. V.29). There has been a tendency among Christian thinkers to elevate this statement of fact into a moral precept and to give self-love the place in Christian ethics that self-realisation had in Greek thought. St Augustine, while admitting that "there is no need of a command that every man should love himself and his own body," yet entitles the relevant chapter; "The command to love God and our neighbour includes a command to love ourselves."[1] Brunner argues that God requires us "to have a grateful love of ourselves. If this command to love ourselves takes a less obvious place in the New Testament it is only because this self-love is assumed as a matter of course, since, indeed, the vital urge leads in this direction."[2] In spite of these and similar opinions in other Christian moralists like Butler[3] and Kierkegaard,[4] our Lord's own sayings convince us that a command to self-love is no integral part of His teaching. After all He was quoting an ancient law from Leviticus, and He knew as well as we do that men have a natural love for themselves. He was probably doing what a modern

---

[1] Augustine, *De doctrina Christiana*, Bk. I, cap. XXVI, quoted P. Ramsey, *Basic Christian Ethics*, p. 101.

[2] Brunner, *Divine Imperative*, p. 171.

[3] Butler, *Sermons*, III.

[4] S. Kierkegaard, *Philosophical Fragments*, Eng. trans. London 1936, p. 30.

preacher does when, on one occasion, he exhorts his hearers to show the same zeal in Christ's service as they show in the making of money, but on another occasion warns them of the dangers of the love of money. Similarly our Lord could tell men to love their neighbours as themselves without expressing or implying any approval of self-love. Thomas à Kempis in the light of our Lord's clear statements declared self-denial to be the "one thing needful" for the Christian—"that, all else having been relinquished, he should relinquish self, and depart entirely from himself, and retain nothing of private love."[5]

Christian thinkers have felt that a command so contrary to human nature requires some justification, and the second of the great commandments suggests one reason for it—we deny ourselves in order to benefit our neighbours. Luther wrote of this; "God's command drives us to our neighbour. . . . Every one should 'put on' his neighbour, and so conduct himself toward him, as if he himself were in the other's place."[6] Even the religious in enclosed orders explain their austerities as being practised in order to benefit the world outside. "The world stands through the intercession of Christians," said Aristides, and, in a modern novel, the Reverend Mother declares that "the more perfect one became, the more valuable one was to the world."[7] We may feel that self-denial has been carried to excess when the same Reverend Mother suggested during a heat-wave that "we should all unite in offering up what she described as the 'the slight discomfort resulting from the warmth of our holy habit' in reparation for the sins of immodesty committed by people who wear insufficient clothing in the world."[8] Yet to maintain that self-denial is practised only for the sake of the neighbour would leave no difference between the self-denial of humanism and Christian self-denial, for many unbelieving humanitarians have denied themselves in order to benefit others. Of course, this is a worthy Christian motive in the light of the place given in the Bible to love of the neighbour, but it is a fact that neither in our

---

[5] T. à Kempis, *De Imitatione Christi*, Part II, cap. XI.
[6] M. Luther, *Treatise on Christian Liberty*, in *Works*, Muhlenberg Press, VOL. II, p. 342, quoted P. Ramsey, *Basic Christian Ethics*, p. 101.
[7] M. Baldwin, *The Called and the Chosen*, p. 254.
[8] *Op. cit.*, p. 131.

Lord's calls to self-denial nor in St Paul's teaching on our dying so that Christ may live in us is there any reference to the neighbour.

Secular moralists have laid much emphasis on self-denial as a means to self-realisation. The athlete's discipline of his body is a means to bodily perfection and the Hindu yogi's ascetic practices may lead to a kind of spiritual perfection. Monica Baldwin, whose novel we have just quoted, says of the nun's life; "Mortification, far from being the suppression of one's personality and initiative, was self-mastery, acquired through the constant practice of self-denial."[9] St Paul's account of his pommeling his body and subduing it (1 Cor. IX.27) indicates that there is room for such practices in the Christian life. Our Lord, who did not think it wrong to remind His disciples of the rewards they would receive, assured them that the man who loses his life for Christ's sake and the Gospel's will ultimately save it (Mk. VIII.35). Similarly T. S. Eliot makes Becket say; "Those who serve the greater cause may make the cause serve them, Still doing right."[10] This, however, is a very different thing from holding that the sole reason for self-denial is that it leads to self-realisation; that would be to put self in the place of God as the supreme object of our love. Even Butler, who held that self-love in general "leads us to one and the same course of life" as virtue, would give the first place to the love of God.[11]

It is for Christ's sake and the Gospel's that the Christian denies himself, but of this no simple reasoned account can be given in terms of a Utilitarian morality. Obviously we do not benefit God or Christ by our self-denial in the way that we may benefit our neighbours or ourselves, and the command to deny ourselves would still hold even when we cannot see that it is contributing in any way to the glory of God or the spread of the Gospel. At the same time all that has been said in this section reminds us that self-denial must be practised not in isolation as the one thing needful for our salvation, but as part of the whole Christian life and particularly of Christian love.

---

[9] M. Baldwin, *The Called and the Chosen*, p. 112.
[10] T. S. Eliot, *Murder in the Cathedral*, London 1935, p. 45.
[11] Butler, *Sermons*, XIII.

§ 2

Self-denial, first and most obviously, means the denial of all false claims for the self, the recognition of man's finitude and sinfulness, of his complete dependence upon God, and of his insecurity apart from God. In this respect, self-denial is nearly the same as humility and the contrary of pride. St Bernard said that humility is the truth about ourselves, and most modern moralists are at pains to dissociate themselves from the hypocritical meekness of a Uriah Heep or the dishonesty of men with a good opinion of their own virtue declaring that they are miserable sinners. C. S. Lewis says that humility does not mean "pretty women trying to believe they are ugly and clever men trying to believe they are fools."[12] There is a humility which is fitting to men apart from their sinfulness; man is a creature wholly dependent on his Creator, and one whose reasonable service is complete submission to the Will of God; this was the characteristic humility of the sinless Jesus. For the rest of us, humility must include the recognition that we are sinners both as individuals and as involved in the corporate sin of the whole human race, so that even our loftiest aspirations and accomplishments are tainted. To confess that we are miserable sinners does not require an emotional working-up of contrition; it requires a simple and honest facing of the facts.

It was in our Lord's personal contacts with men and women that He led them to humility through seeing the truth about themselves. It sometimes came in a flash of insight in the presence of Christ's holiness, as when St Peter exclaimed; "Depart from me, for I am a sinful man, O Lord" (Lk. v.8), or when Zacchaeus realised that Christ's presence challenged him to make restitution for all his exactions (Lk. xix.1-9). It sometimes came in plain, outspoken speech as when Jesus called St Peter Satan (Mk. viii.33), or when he told the Samaritan woman the straight facts of her condition (Jn. iv.17-18). It may have come with more than a touch of humour when our Lord gave to His disciples nicknames like "sons of thunder" (Mk. iii.17). It is still part of the duty of Christian preachers to present the Jesus of the Gospels in such a way that

[12] C. S. Lewis, *The Screwtape Letters*, London 1942, p. 73.

their hearers, seeing themselves in the light of His holiness, learn humility.

Self-love does not only pervert a man's view of himself; it gives him a wrong view of the whole world. " A man regards as real a world which gives him most compensation and in which his self-love feels least wounded. . . . Self-love creates a phantasmagorical world of its own in which all realities are misplaced."[13] The political attitudes of our time are often too obviously determined by our own self-love; the Germans have been transformed from brutal Nazis to staunch defenders of freedom because their place in the NATO alliance gives confidence to our self-love. We can only see the real political situation when we regain "a spiritually enlightened view of the world," and this is the view where God is at the centre, and self and its interests are denied.

The present century is often hailed as the century of the greatest human achievements, but it is also the century in which the limitations of human accomplishment have been most clearly displayed. We think of Hegel's picture of the modern State as the culmination of the history of the human spirit, and then of the terrible outcomes of that theory in National Socialism and Leninism-Stalinism. We think of the marvellous advances of physical science, and of their outcome in Hiroshima. We think of the profundities of depth psychology and of their outcomes in brain-washing and in helplessness in face of juvenile delinquency. It would be foolish to deny the real benefits men have gained from the extension of human knowledge, but any honest man facing the facts of today must admit that they do not supply the "one thing needful" for our civilisation. Our exaltation of these things is also part of our self-love, and it is only by denying the claims of the self that we shall realise that it is by the grace of God that men can be saved in such a way as to make a right use of the achievements of science.

§ 3

Self-denial means, again, the ignoring of the self and its interests—what is best described in modern idiom as self-forgetfulness. The modern use of the word "self-denial" for

[13] N. Berdyaev, *The Destiny of Man*, London 1937, p. 230 f.

abstinence from certain luxuries, for example during Lent, or
for certain ascetic practices, is altogether wrong. It is equally
wrong to link renunciation of the self too closely with renunciation of the life of society or of material goods, as Romanist
theologians tend to do.[14] Christian renunciation of family ties
or of wealth has for most Christians only the character of a
preference;[15] they must give these things second place to the
claims of Christ, and only those entering a religious order are
called to renounce them altogether. The denial of self is, on
the other hand, a renunciation commanded by Christ on every
man who would be His disciple. It is here indeed that the
difference lies between ordinary religious asceticism and the
distinctive asceticism of the Christian. It was a scandal to
religious people that Jesus came eating and drinking—a friend
of publicans and sinners. For the conventional kind of
asceticism Jesus had very little use. When Mary of Bethany
poured her expensive flask of perfume on His head, Jesus
apparently found a real joy in the gift, and reproved those who
recommended a more ascetic use of the perfume (Mk. xiv.3-9).
The danger of an asceticism which emphasises doing without
pleasant things is that, so far from helping us to deny self, it
concentrates the mind on the self. Success in ascetic practices,
as spiritual directors have long realised, easily leads to spiritual
pride—what Bonhoeffer calls "the flagrant spiritual self-
assertion of the religious."[16] Instead of finding security and
self-satisfaction in his possessions like the worldly man, the
ascetic may find security in the merit of his self-sacrifice and
pride in his self-mortification. True Christian asceticism gets
away from self because the mind of the Christian is set on
the things that are above, on the Kingdom of God and His
righteousness. It is possible by God's grace for men living
a busy life in the world still to forget themselves, and rich
men appear to have accomplished the feat of which the
camel is incapable in connexion with the eye of a needle.
The interest of such men is not in their riches, and, what is
even more important, not in themselves; they have denied

---

[14] E.g. Lebreton, "Renoncement dans le N.T."

[15] *Op. cit.*, p. 377.

[16] D. Bonhoeffer, *The Cost of Discipleship*, London 1938, p. 41. Translation of
Nachfolge, Munich 1937.

themselves and taken up the Cross, and they are truly children of the Kingdom.

There are human means of forgetting self, and Christian ethics never despises such means, although it realises their subordinate place in the Christian life. Thomas Chalmers spoke of "the expulsive power of a new affection," and, outside the Christian faith, enthusiasm for a great cause is the way in which some of the greatest heroes of history from Pericles to Gandhi have in some measure forgotten themselves. Yet the danger here is very great of such a man so identifying his cause with himself that the cynical may suspect that in his self-sacrifice for the cause he is really glorifying himself and ministering to his self-love. This is the special temptation of the zealous Christian, perhaps particularly of ministers and missionaries. We give ourselves enthusiastically to work for Christ and the Gospel, but how insidiously do our enthusiasms come to be motivated by the fact that this is *our* piece of work, and not by the fact that it is Christ's work. In the mission field, a missionary is tempted to resist the closing or transformation of an institution with which he himself has been long identified, although it may be evident to the unprejudiced observer that the day of its evangelistic usefulness is over. It may be that even St Paul, the greatest of all fellow workers with Christ, found it difficult at one stage of his life not to give himself too large a place in his mission. St Paul's own honour sometimes appears to be part of his concern for the cause of Christ, but one of the wonderful things about the imprisonment epistles is that they show how the aged St Paul had forgotten himself and passed beyond the stage of vindicating himself as well as his mission. God has by His grace done something very great to a man who, contrary to his natural temperament, so learns to forget himself, for self-forgetfulness is something that is not attained by moral effort.

There are two Christian enthusiasms where this danger is less, and we have referred to them already as motives to self-denial—the love of one's neighbour and the love of God in Christ. Even the Christian who may be tempted in human weakness to use an institution or a cause or even a congregation (impersonally conceived) as a means to his own self-love, would reject as utterly base the idea of using his friend or his Master in this way. Two of the heroes of the 1939 war, both now ministers of the Church of Scotland, were Donald Smith, who wrote *And All the Trumpets*,[17] and Donald Caskie, who wrote *The Tartan Pimpernel*.[18] Both books are stories of heroic adventure under conditions of appalling danger and temptation. Yet what comes out most vividly in both books is the whole-hearted concern and love of both authors for their comrades, something secondary only to their common love for Christ. The result is that, in writing their autobiographies—an activity in which most men display consciously or unconsciously self-love at its worst—both these Christian men actually deny themselves. This was, of course, due to love of Christ as well as love of comrade, and this leads us deeper into the nature of self-denial.

§ 4

Self-denial in the New Testament is more than humility, more than self-forgetfulness. Our Lord's challenge to a would-be follower is to "deny himself and *take up his cross* and follow me" (Mk. VIII.34), or to "*bear his own cross* and come after me" (Lk. XIV.27).[19] The carrying of a cross seems to be an integral part of self-denial and an indispensable condition of discipleship. St Paul uses similar language, more definitely linked with what happened at Calvary; "We have died with Christ" (Rom. VI.8); "I have been crucified with Christ; it is no longer I who live, but Christ who lives in me" (Gal. II.20).

We who glory in the Cross of Christ, see it in the perspective of Christ's glorious victory over sin and death; this outlook has already begun in the Fourth Gospel which sees Christ being lifted up on the Cross as part of His exaltation. When Jesus, however, spoke to His disciples some time before Calvary about their carrying a cross—and the frequency of its repetition makes it almost certain that this is an authentic saying of Jesus—the Cross was not yet "towering o'er the wrecks of Time" with "all the light of sacred story gathering round its head sublime."[20] When Jesus was speaking, the thoughts of

---

[17] J. D. Smith, *And All the Trumpets*, London 1954.

[18] D. C. Caskie, *The Tartan Pimpernel*, London 1957.

[19] Principal J. E. Davey has drawn my attention to Torrey's suggestion that in the original Aramaic Jesus bade His disciples to take up His *yoke*; cf. Mt. XI.29.

[20] *Church Hymnary*, no. 113.

His disciples must have gone to violent criminals or misguided fanatics of the Resistance Movement, who went on their last humiliating journey carrying the heavy cross-bar of the instrument of their execution. Our thoughts might similarly go to Jews in Hitler's Germany wearing compulsorily the yellow badge of the star of David as they were driven to their mass executions. Jesus offered to His disciples all the hardships and sufferings that a Garibaldi or a Churchill offered in their own days with little of the heroic pageantry that they wove into their words. If Jesus did speak of His rising again, the disciples obviously did not take it in, and they had no vision then of the joy that was set before Him. Before Calvary the cross meant death and nothing else to its victims. "No one denies himself unless, out of loyalty to Jesus, he accepts death in advance, even the most ignominious death."[21] The man following Christ in Britain today does not think of himself as accepting the possibility of martyrdom, but many of our own generation have done so.

It was, however, before his death as a martyr, while he was still living a busy life in the world, that St Paul wrote; "I am crucified with Christ." We try to soften this saying by interpreting it to mean that the sinful element in us must die. Of course it must, as St Paul makes clear in Romans VI, but it means also that "our personality as a whole must pass through death. . . . We are seriously bidden to despair of ourselves."[22] The reason for this dying may well be that the self is so impregnated with moral evil that it has to be put to death and buried in such a way that its very existence can be denied. Yet, as our Lord's own teaching suggests, getting rid of the devil that is self may leave the house of the soul empty and ready to be occupied by seven worse devils. "We ought not," writes Jules Lebreton, "to remain without attachment to anything or anybody." If we do that, "we are in danger of letting the whole territory that has been saved from our natural passions be invaded by egoism and sloth."[23] Self-denial is the making of room for Christ in us.

---

[21] C. Masson, "Cross," in *Vocabulary of the Bible*, ed. J. J. von Allmen, p. 76.
[22] Brunner, *Divine Imperative*, p. 174.
[23] Lebreton, "Renoncement dans le N.T," p. 412 (my translation).

We are passing beyond the sphere of ethics.   To take up one's cross is no mere moral imitation of the self-sacrifice of Christ, no simple receiving of a moral strength won for us through the death of our Saviour, no ascetic mortification of the flesh through which we share in the sufferings of Jesus. All these things may have a place in Christian practice, but they do not add up to St Paul's experience of being crucified with Christ so that "it is no longer I who live but Christ who lives in me."   We may think that this experience can only be expressed in sacramental or mystical language, and St Paul uses both (e.g. Rom. vi.4; Gal. ii.20), and that it has nothing to do with morality.   Bonhoeffer, who speaks with the authority of one himself facing martyrdom for the cause of Christ, writes of the man who has this experience; "Jesus Christ lives for him and in him, and . . . Jesus Christ occupies within him exactly the space which was previously occupied by his own knowledge of good and evil."[24]   St Paul never forgets the moral implications of this transformation; the man who is in Christ is "a new creation" morally (ii Cor. v.17); the baptised person cannot continue in sin (Rom. vi.4); those who have died and whose life is hid with Christ in God must put to death all the vices of unregenerate mankind (Col. iii.3-5).

The holiness of Christ in us is a different kind of holiness from the natural knowledge of good and evil.   It belongs to Christ and not to us so that "for the Christian there is and can be no private holiness."[25]   It is in the unity of Christ's body, the Church, that this holiness is manifested to the world. This is a fact that we do recognise negatively; "if one member suffers, all suffer together" (i Cor. xii.26), and the moral lapse of one member is a reason for repentance in the whole Church (i Cor. v.2).   Yet we scarcely grasp the positive truth that there is in the Church as a whole a new kind of holiness—the love that transcends all human morality, because it is patterned on the mutual love of the Father and the Son (Jn. xvii.26). Those who regard the only function of the Church as the saving of their own souls, even although they interpret that salvation in terms of the highest moral achievements, are not denying themselves.

[24] Bonhoeffer, *Ethics*, p. 165.
[25] Brunner, *Divine Imperative*, p. 177.

Yet the Christian's self-denial cannot mean that he becomes a mere cog in the ecclesiastical machine, or even a cell in the Body of Christ quite indistinguishable from other cells. To suppose this would give the Church the same impersonal character which all our moral instincts find so repugnant in the totalitarian state or in the large industrial unit of modern capitalism. The challenge of our time, we think, is not to eliminate individual differences, but to foster the distinctiveness of different personalities each with a separate gift to give to the social groups to which they belong. This sounds more like self-realisation than self-denial, but there are two qualifications. The more one forgets oneself in love and service within the Body, the more are the true potentialities of one's being realised and fulfilled; "he who loses his life . . . will find it" (Mt. x.39). Of course it should be our aim in a Christian society that every other social unit, political and industrial, should in this respect mirror the life of the Church. Again the importance of the individual within the Church, should, like the importance of little children, be something of which the individual himself is unaware. The churchman who thinks himself indispensable is a peril to the holiness of the Church.

§ 5

Self-denial differs from love, the other great characteristic of the Christian life, in that while every one approves of love, however much they misunderstand it, few approve of self-denial. Realists regard self-denial as a quality quite unsuited to life in a competitive world, where a man needs to assert himself in order to reap life's richest rewards. Such people might admit that there are, even in modern society, a few advantages for the humble man, the man who knows his own limitations, and even for the man who sometimes thinks of others, if it be only his own family, rather than of himself. They recognise too the value of the so-called self-denial that has in view some future gain for the self, and more enlightened humanists accept self-denial in so far as it is a means to the service of others and to one's own self-realisation. Such self-denial, they would affirm, must never be carried too far, and the man who does so is simply destroying himself. The danger for the Christian is that he may mistake this prudential self-denial for the self-denial enjoined by Christ.

When, however, as in this study, we see self-denial not as a matter of moral endeavour, but as the inevitable moral implication of the Cross of Christ, self-denial is no longer regarded only as a means; it is the essence of the Christian life. Some Christians who have realised this most fully, chiefly within the Roman Church, have made the mistake of supposing that the best, if not the only way of sharing in the Cross of Christ, is by practising the austerities of the religious life of a monastic community. It was not in this ascetic way that our Lord Himself practised self-denial, and it is not thus that the majority of Christians are called to practise it in the world of the twentieth century. Indeed, if our argument is right, self-denial is not so much a matter of effort in practice as of receiving what Christ has done for us within His Body, the Church. Even within the Church, we are only likely to deny ourselves when we learn that other and greatest of Christian virtues, the love of God and of our neighbours, for it is only as the love of God floods our hearts that we forget and deny ourselves in true Christian fashion.

Literature

J. BUTLER, *Fifteen Sermons preached at the Rolls Chapel* in *Works*, ed. W. E. Gladstone, London 1896, VOL. II, Sermons III and XII.

E. BRUNNER, *The Divine Imperative*, London 1937, ch. XVII.

P. RAMSEY, *Basic Christian Ethics*, London 1953, pp. 92-103.

C. MASSON, "Cross," in *Vocabulary of the Bible*, ed. J. J. von Allmen, London 1958, pp. 73-7. Translation of *Vocabulaire biblique*, 2nd edn. Neuchâtel and Paris 1956.

D. BONHOEFFER, *The Cost of Discipleship*, London 1948. Translation of *Nachfolge*, Munich 1937.

J. LEBRETON, "La doctrine du renoncement dans le Nouveau Testament," in *Nouvelle revue théologique*, LXV (1938), pp. 385-412.

Chapter XV

The Christian Conception of Love

ALL Christian love has its source and exemplar in the love of God. "Beloved," wrote St John, "if God so loved us, we also ought to love one another" (1 Jn. IV.11), or again: "God is love, and he who abides in love abides in God, and God abides in him" (1 Jn. IV.16). St Paul was equally clear; it is God's love which "has been poured into our hearts through the Holy Spirit which has been given to us" (Rom. v.5), and it is the love of Christ (which is, of course, the love of God revealed in Christ) that constrains us to live no longer for ourselves (II Cor. v.14)—the usual way in which our human love is evidenced. Dietrich Bonhoeffer echoed this from his German prison; "No one knows what love is except in the self-revelation of God. . . . It is only the concrete action and suffering of . . . Jesus Christ which will make it possible to understand what love is."[1] So we must begin with the love of God; and yet our understanding of God's love comes to us through the experience of human love. It was with a picture of an earthly father, surrounded by the human things of home and field, calves and kids, robes and rings, sons and servants, that Jesus made His most vivid portrait of the love of God; and it was not only in dying on Calvary, but also in living in human fellowship with Peter and John, Martha and Mary that Jesus Himself exhibited the Father's love to men. Yet while Christ gave the supreme revelation of that love, we need not despise the lesser revelations of it that come to us in our ordinary human experience; a man may truly say that, in the forgiveness given to him by a man or a woman, he has gained a new understanding of the love of God. In any systematic treatment of our subject, the love of God must come first, for it is logically

[1] Bonhoeffer, *Ethics*, p. 173 f.

and actually prior to all human loves, but in our own experience the love of a parent or of a friend may be the step by
which we have risen to some understanding of God's love.

The essential characteristic of the love of God, which we
may call by its biblical name of *agape* to distinguish it from
forms of love that may appear different, is self-giving. The
Swedish theologian, Nygren, contrasted *agape* with *eros*, the
love about which the Greeks talked much, in this respect among
others, that *eros* is egocentric: "Every desire of the self is a
desire of good for the self."[2] This cannot be accepted as true
of all human love, apart from the *agape* that is poured into
men's hearts through the Holy Spirit; the pagan mother and
the pagan lover may forget themselves in their desire for the
good of those they love. What is true is that a great deal of
ordinary human love is selfish, and seeks to find satisfaction
for its own desires in the beloved person or object, and that in
the loves of fallen men there is always a trace of self-regard.
Karl Barth also regards *agape* as self-giving, "a turning from
self to another for the sake of the other."[3] The fact that God
is love indicates that the giving of the self for the sake of another
is not something occasionally necessary to meet adverse conditions like a "national emergency." It is something essential
to the nature of the universe, found eternally in God Himself.
An obvious manifestation of it in nature, animal as well as
human, is the maternal instinct by which the mother gives
herself up, sometimes even sacrificing her life, for the sake of her
young. Our Lord saw something of the same kind in the corn
of wheat dying and bearing much fruit (Jn. xii.24). (Modern
biological study may complicate, but it does not invalidate the
point of, this example.) In the world's history, the supreme
example of this is the Cross of Jesus Christ, and this demonstrates
the special form the love of God had to take in dealing with sinful
men, for in the love at work on the Cross men have found
forgiveness, reconciliation, and restoration. Our Christian
reaction is: "He loved me, and gave Himself for me" (Gal.
ii.20). Forgiveness, which is essentially love restored, seems

---

[2] A. Nygren, *Agape and Eros*, London 1937, VOL. I, p. 137. Translation of
Den kristna kärlekstanken, Stockholm 1930.

[3] G. W. Bromiley, "The doctrine of reconciliation," henceforth cited as
"Reconciliation," in *Scottish Journal of Theology*, x (1957), p. 84.

to us in our need the very essence of the love of God, but His love is found in Creation and Providence as well as in Redemption. God is always the God who gives, but on the Cross in a special way He gave Himself for the sake of men to bring them back to His love.

Nygren lays great emphasis on the fact that *agape* is spontaneous, uncaused or unmotivated. "God's love is 'uncaused,' not of course in the sense that it is arbitrary or capricious; on the contrary, it is necessary, because it belongs to the very nature of God Himself. Again, God's love is always spontaneous; it is not called out by anything outside itself. Hence, when it is said that God loves man, this is not a judgment on what man is like, but on what God is like."[4] This states the obvious truth that the love of God is not given to a man because of any merit in that man; it is certainly wrong to think that God loves the godly on account of his godliness.[5] In this respect the *agape* of God is far more like our ordinary human love than the more refined *eros* of the Greek philosophers. For it is to something worthy, to the beauty in a person or object, that Plato's *eros* is drawn: "that which is the object of love must indeed be fair, and delicate, and perfect, and most happy."[6] In common life, very fortunately for many of us, people can and do love those who are neither fair nor perfect. A mother loves her deformed and difficult child, and outsiders often wonder what two very ordinary lovers see in one another to love. God's *agape*, however, is not uncaused and spontaneous in the sense of being indifferent as to its object. We must not think of love as an emanation or a substance necessarily flowing out from God whether there be an object to receive it or not, like the water which must spray from a fountain in all directions with no concern as to the objects on which it falls. Barth's analysis suggests an important safeguard here; *agape* is self-giving *for the sake of* the other. Nygren is certainly right that this does not mean "for the sake of the merit or worth of the other," but love is still for the sake of the other even when there is no merit in the other. The teaching of the Bible is most helpful here; we may smile a little at the pictures of God

---

[4] Nygren, *Agape and Eros*, VOL. I, p. 52.
[5] *Op. cit.*, VOL. I, p. 54.
[6] Plato, *Symposium*, 204.

providing garments for Adam and Eve, suddenly embarrassed by the consciousness of their own bodies, or of His visiting Abraham in his tent by the oak of Mamre in order to discuss family matters with him, but the truth behind these stories is that it is in the concrete affairs of men, the things that concern men most, that the love of God is at work. The climax of the revelation is One who went about doing good, particularly concerned with human need, and finally sharing a gallows with two criminals. To call love "uncaused" may lead us to forget that there is no love without an object, and the objects of God's love, so far as we are concerned and our knowledge goes, are just sinful men and women for whom love must show itself as forgiveness. The Bible does talk of God loving righteousness and hating iniquity, just as we talk of people loving the ballet and hating Communism, but both these uses are secondary and metaphorical; it is men and women whom God loves and we love.

This raises the question, "Does God love all men or does He love only a limited group—the elect or the true Israel or the like?" Is God's love what Karl Barth calls "an electing love"?[7] It is common today to take the universality of God's love for granted—that all men are His children, so that "the dear Lord, who loveth us, He made and loveth all." (Coleridge, quite logically, includes birds and beasts, as well as all mankind, within God's love.) Yet the Bible clearly indicates that God has a special love for His own people. Malachi hears God saying, "Yet I have loved Jacob, but I have hated Esau" (Mal. 1.2-3). ("Hate" here may be the vivid Eastern way of expressing a love that comes second.)[8] In Hosea, we have a picture of God's special love to Israel in terms both of loving husband (e.g. Hos. 11.19-20) and devoted parent (e.g. Hos. XI.3-4). Even in the Gospel where we are told that "God so loved the world" (and the "world" in the most common Johannine usage is the world alienated from God), we are also told how Christ, who was the revelation of God, had a special love to a brother and two sisters at Bethany (Jn. XI.5), and to one of His immediate disciples (Jn. XIII.23).

Are we then to conclude that *agape*, as applied even to God,

---

[7] Bromiley, "Reconciliation," p. 84.
[8] Cf. Gen. XXIX.31; Lk. XIV.26.

is an ambiguous word, that there is one *agape* given to all men without distinction, and another *agape*, more akin to our human love, which God felt towards the patriarchs and Christ gave to a few selected people? We may parody Kipling and say: "God gave all men all men to love, But since our hearts are small, Ordained for each a few should prove, Beloved over all." This is certainly true of us, and it may be that, in the limitations of His human life, Christ could only give a close personal friendship to a small number of people. But, quite certainly, this does not apply to the love of God the Father, who is subject to no such limitations. The common, and, in my opinion, the thoroughly wrong way of meeting this difficulty is to suppose that, while God loves all men, He "liked" the patriarchs or the people of Israel with an affection closely resembling human love as we ordinarily think of it, but really having nothing to do with the Divine *agape*. Similarly, while the *agape* of Jesus towards all men was such that He died to save them from their sins, He liked a few human individuals in the way that we love our friends. If, however, God's *agape* is the source and pattern of our love to one another as Christians, it must have its supreme expression in close personal relations —relations like those human ones where we expect liking as well as forgiveness and self-giving. The fact to be taken seriously here is the fact of election,[9] that God chooses a particular race or a particular individual for a special purpose. God called Israel out of the world to bring the world unto Himself. Such an election of Israel was bound to bring the people of Israel into personal relations with God, and once men are into the sphere of personal relations, *agape* will show the personal interest, the emotional warmth, and the genuine liking that we usually associate with love. Abraham, who was the first of the race to know God's electing purpose according to the record, became "the friend of God;" Israel became "my chosen in whom my soul delights." We must not confine the *agape* of God to those whose election to a special destiny brings them into special relations with Him. We may see a picture of the *agape* of God in the story of the Good Samaritan. He may or may not have had a benevolent attitude to the Jewish race as such,

[9] For a discussion of this see H. H. Rowley, *The Biblical Doctrine of Election*, London 1950.

M

but it was when he came into personal contact with the wounded Jew on the road that there was the self-giving of *agape*. It is wrong to think of the Samaritan as using the wounded Jew as a means of expressing the *agape* that filled his soul; the compassion of the Samaritan, which is recorded in the story, was an emotion felt towards this particular person, and indeed a rudimentary love. There may be a sense in which the *agape* of God is infinite and universal, but the *agape* which concerns us is the forgiving and active love, which God shows in His personal dealings with men, whether it be an individual clearly chosen for a special task or a poor sufferer encountered on the wayside, when the *agape* of God has all the concrete warmth and individual concern of our human love at its best. To deny this would be to make the love of God in certain respects a poorer thing than the love of man. How God chooses those to whom He makes known His love is beyond our understanding.

Some thinkers find a difference between God's *agape* and ordinary human love in the fact that *agape* creates in the object of love something worthy to be loved, particularly the restored image of God in forgiven sinners. This is, however, subject to our human limitations, sometimes true even of ordinary human love. It is a happy experience that, when a woman falls in love with a man, she sometimes evokes in him lovable qualities that previously were invisible or perhaps even did not exist. The same creativity can be seen in the love given by parents to their children, although here the slowness of the child's development makes the process less obvious. "The best modern psychiatry, when dealing with the problem of delinquency in children . . . insists that they must be accepted, must find security in the love of others, out of which security they gain sufficient freedom from self to "let go" and love others."[10] This is a picture of the security which sinning men need to find in the love of God, so that they can "let go" in their own creative urges. The stories of the saints are, for the most part, stories of men who with some reason thought of themselves as the chief of sinners, but in whom holiness and love itself were created by the *agape* of God. This is one of the paradoxes of the love of God. God loves us as sinners, and

[10] Niebuhr, *Christian Realism*, p. 145.

"shows His love for us in that while we we were yet sinners, Christ died for us" (Rom. v.8), but, in responding to that love, we are "called to be saints" (Rom. 1.7). Holiness, or moral worth, is not the cause of God's loving us, but it is certainly the effect of God's loving us. We do not understand how *agape* creates goodness; the most comprehensible analogies are in the creativities of human love.

There are other qualities attributed to God in the Bible which we understand by the analogy of our human qualities, particularly the justice and holiness of God. In the Christian revelation, indeed, love in its work of forgiving appears to take precedence of and even comprehend justice and holiness, and we never can believe that God possesses them in such a way as would detract from His love. The very fact that God loves men means that He deals with them as men, and not as puppets or animal pets, and, in such dealings there must be justice and holiness. The New Testament saying; "The Lord disciplines him whom he loves" (Heb. xii.6), reminds us that the sterner dealings of God with men are the actions of God's love as well as of His holiness and justice. Our human love to one another, if it is to follow the example of the Divine *agape*, must exhibit in proper proportion God's holiness and God's justice.

§ 2

Love begets love, and the response to the *agape* of God to man should be the love of man to God. St Paul, however, never speaks explicitly of man's *agape* to God; for him "faith" seems to be the more appropriate word for our human response. This is certainly not surprising; it might appear blasphemous to use the same word for the perfect love of God and the warped, mixed-up aspirations of sinful men. There is a sense, indeed, in which men ought to fear God in His Divine Majesty. "The fear of the Lord is the beginning of wisdom" (Prov. ix.10), and even St John, who knows that the ultimate goal is that we should love God somewhat in the way that He loves us, seems to suggest that there must be an educative process in which "perfect love casts out fear" (1 Jn. iv.18). But even when this is accomplished, there must still be some differences between God's love for man and man's love for God. God cannot love

us for our moral worth, but we can assuredly love God for His
moral worth. God's love creates what is worthy in the object
of His love; there can be no such direct creation of worth in
our love to God. And gratitude for what God had done for us
in Christ must always be central in our love to Him.

There is a barrier of ignorance and sin on man's part which
seems to prevent any real possibility of his loving God.
"Obviously we cannot love someone we do not know; therefore," suggests a modern devotional book, "our first effort must
be to know God."[11] This is to begin at the wrong end, for
Christ has broken down the barrier, reconciling us to God,
and in Himself showing us God as a Person whom we can
know and love. "He came down from heaven, in perfect
love from Perfect Love, and became man for us men and our
salvation." So, as soon as Barth points out that love for God
includes love for Jesus, he "retracts his own earlier exclusion of
emotional warmth."[12] We are most of us like the child who
says that he loves Jesus but is afraid of God. Indeed there is a
danger of our love for the man Jesus degenerating into a
sentimental hero-worship. But, as we grow to know Him
better not only as man but as Lord and God, something happens
to us and to our love. Our natural human love by God's grace
begins to take on something of the quality of the Divine *agape*.
St Augustine, who thought much on this, has made it very
clear that it is only by the grace which God gives to us in His
dealings with us that He raises our natural love to a love that is
more fitting to offer to God. "When God gives Himself to us
in Christ, He gives us at once the object we are to love and the
Caritas with which to love it."[13] In Christ our love to God is not
merely a love at the human level to which He came down from
heaven; it is through our communion with Him being transformed into love at the Divine level to which He has ascended
to be the first among many brethren (Heb. II.10). This transformation is the work of the Holy Spirit speaking to us of
Christ (Jn. XVI.14).

We have to keep together two complementary truths
about our relationships to God. Man is made in the image and

---

[11] G. Bowden, *The Dazzling Darkness*, London 1950, p. 39.
[12] Bromiley, "Reconciliation," p. 84.
[13] Nygren, *Agape and Eros*, VOL. II, p. 307.

likeness of God.   He is not merely a creature like the other things which God has made;   in the jargon of Buber and Heim, God addresses man as a "Thou" and not as an "It."   Man, too, is in a covenant relationship with God.   It is true that God always takes the initiative in making the covenant and that man depends on God for the power he needs to fulfil his part. Yet man is a party to the covenant, one who can respond to God in love and obedience.   Yet man, even when "ransomed, healed, restored, forgiven," remains God's creature.   The love he gives to God must be like the love of a child to his father, never the love of a man to his brother or friend.

Man's response of love to God has certain resemblances to one aspect of *eros* in Greek thought.   In Plato, *eros* is the love for the Beautiful and the Good and the way of man to the Divine.[14]   Human nature does have such lofty aspirations, although many think of them as so self-centred and acquisitive that they can have nothing to do with the love that should be man's response to God's *agape*.   The Christian tradition from Augustine onwards to the Reformation was rather that the *agape* of God takes hold of the natural aspiration of man towards what is above him, and transforms it into the likeness of the Divine *agape*.   By *eros* all men look up to God and seek Him, but such is man's weakness that all his efforts are unavailing. The bent will must be straightened and then uplifted, and for this God's descent to man and His grace are necessary.[15] "Grace does not destroy all that is human; it perfects it and elevates it to a new dynamic".[16]   It is wrong to think of the Christian's love to God as having no roots in that *eros* through which, with many illusions and perversions, men have aspired to what is above.   Such aspirations Christianity does not destroy, but fulfil.

We cannot make the sharp contrast that Nygren has made between *agape* and *eros* in the respect that *eros* is a will to have and to possess.[17]   The language of non-Christian mystics often suggests the desire not to have and to possess the Divine Being, but to be possessed by Him and to surrender oneself wholly

[14] Plato, *Symposium*, 204.
[15] M. D'Arcy, *The Mind and Heart of Love*, London 1945, p. 67.
[16] *Op. cit.*, p. 71.
[17] Nygren, *Agape and Eros*, VOL. I. p. 165.

to Him.   When such mysticism uses the language of sexual love, the soul is the bride waiting to be possessed by the divine bridegroom.   Similarly the first response to the love of God in Christ is the readiness to receive Him, to open the door of the heart to Him, to say with Mary: "Be it unto me according to Thy word."   Even when the outcome of our receiving the love of God through the Holy Spirit is the active giving of ourselves for the sake of our fellow men, it is still true to say that we are being moved by the love of God rather than that we are the active agents ourselves.

§ 3

The love of man to man is something so familiar that we may fail to notice its rich variety.   What is common to our various loves appears to be a state of feeling, and the endeavours that theologians have undertaken to make love a matter of will and so of moral duty seem misdirected towards the perversion of language.   (In the *Shorter Oxford English Dictionary*, for example, the emotive element appears to be the primary one in all the meanings given for "love" outside the game of tennis!)   Yet the theologians are drawing attention to something that is undoubtedly true of love in its higher forms;   it involves a man's whole being, knowledge and will as well as emotion. The Hebrew idiom of a man "knowing" his wife suggests something larger than the sexual act, and the Johannine teaching makes the knowledge of God almost equivalent to abiding in God's love (e.g. Jn. xvii.26).   The Bible is even more clear that love finds expression in willing and action; the loving of God means the obeying of His commandments (1 Jn. v.3).   Yet here, too, the emotional element is central; it is because there is no friction between duty and inclination in the loving heart that "love is the fulfilling of the law."[18]

The rich varieties of love are illustrated but by no means exhausted in the uses of the Greek word *eros*.   *Eros* obviously belongs to what we may call the instinctive make-up of our human nature, the kind of thing that modern psychologists find in the depths of the unconscious.   It occurs in love between the sexes, but Plato, like too many since, tends to brush this

[18] Niebuhr, *Christian Realism*, p. 140.

aside as "vulgar love,"[19] identifying it with its perversion lust. *Eros* is again the desire to possess or to take to oneself what is worthy in an object, and so the desire for the Good or the Beautiful, which is part of our instinctive nature. Even in pagan man, however, love is not confined to those persons or objects in which he sees a goodness or a beauty to be possessed. It may be true that we needs must love the highest that we know, but we love a great many other things as well. Of this "heavenly love," as Plato calls it, the supreme form is the love of God to which we have already referred. What is strangely lacking in the common analysis of love in terms of *eros* is what we may call the love of the natural relationships. There is a love of parent to child, of child to parent, of brother to sister, and, less obviously, even of servant to master, of master to servant, and of neighbour to neighbour. There is a love that can be traced to natural ties, as well as the loves that come from sexual attraction and the recognition of attractive qualities and mutual sympathy. "I know that personal relations are the real life for ever and ever," says one of the characters in E. M. Forster's *Howard's End*,[20] and personal relations are just those that are (we may believe), in the order of creation as God intended it to be, characterised by love; the purpose of the feeling of love may well be to preserve the natural orders and make them agreeable to God's creatures. When love is lacking, our natural relationships go wrong. For completeness here we must mention the love of friendship or *philia*. It differs from the love of natural relationships in being a matter of deliberate choice; we are born with our relatives, we choose our friends. There may accordingly be often an erotic element in friendship in that we may choose a friend because of some attractive quality in him. What is evident in friendship is what may be called the mutuality of love; it takes two to make friends more truly than to make a quarrel, and a love that meets no response is a truncated love.

We may well believe that in the Divine intention all these varieties of love were to be characterised by the "giving of oneself for the sake of the other" which we know in the revealed *agape* of God. Indeed, even among pagans we often find a

---

[19] Plato, *Symposium*, 181.
[20] Quoted Bowden, *The Dazzling Darkness*, p. 112.

great deal of such self-giving between husband and wife, in the relationships of the home, and even among neighbours; people who live in reasonable harmony together must to some extent give as well as take. This is also true of the heavenly *eros*; the lover of beauty has, in some sense, to surrender himself to the beauty he pursues, and the scientist has to make real sacrifices in his enterprise of discovering the truth. The descriptions of *eros* as "egocentric," "a form of self-assertion," or "a will to have and possess resting on a sense of need,"[21] while they may draw attention to dangers that are implicit in our human love, are simply not true of a great deal of human love, even apart from its transformation by the grace of God in Christ.

What is true is that in all its forms love is impaired, perverted, and destroyed by human sin, and particularly by human selfishness. It may be that in the very ecstasy and spontaneity that are characteristic of love there are the beginnings of danger; excess, as Jean Guitton points out, seems to be "love's desirable and normal course,"[22] and this may lead to the uncontrolled excesses of savage delight which Euripides pictures in the *Bacchae*, or to the idolatry which gives to the human beloved a love of which only the Divine Being is worthy, as in the romances of chivalry. Love may be perverted again by a too prudent consideration of its appropriate objects and its consequences; the home can become a nucleus for bourgeois self-centredness, and the wounded man on the road to Jericho may be seen merely as one who might disturb the pattern of one's religious life. It is easy for our love to lose all traces of the glory and wonder of the *agape* in which it was created.

There is a perversion of love which is so common that men have taken it to be the essence of *eros*. The lover treats the object of his love not as a person but as a thing—a means to his own enjoyment or self-enhancement. There is, indeed, alongside our natural tendency to self-giving, a tendency to regard the self as of primary importance and to use other things as means to the good of the self. Human experience, however, should have taught us that the human spirit can never be

[21] Nygren, *Agape and Eros*, VOL. I, p. 165.
[22] J. Guitton, *Essay on Human Love*, London 1951, p. 20. Translation of *Essai sur l'amour humain*, Paris 1948.

content with things, or even with persons used as things or means. Ecclesiastes contains the biblical revelation of the futility of such an attempt. "It [the human I] will seek—and it is not some *other thing* which it will seek, for things cannot interest it nor satisfy it—it will seek *another* I, which it will long to make its own in order to discover itself there and to lose itself. . . . To be a person is essentially to be in search of a person."[23] Moralists have expressed this by saying that we must treat other persons as ends and not as means, or they have laid down principles of distributive and retributive justice, which secure "a tolerable harmony of life with life," but are only preliminary conditions for the presence of love. What may happen thereafter, when one person faces another as a person, without seeking gain or advantage for the self from the other, has traditionally been described as having a supernatural origin, whether it be an arrow from Cupid's quiver or *agape* poured into men's hearts by the Spirit of God. "*Agape* enters from another dimension into the whole of life, and into all qualities of love."[24] Unfortunately, when this happens, it does not guarantee that there is no further danger of treating the loved one as a means. Love given unselfishly in a spirit of high adventure may degenerate into a desire for the comfort or self-seeking of the one-time lover. The wife may become a cheap housekeeper; the friend may become a tool in winning wealth or power, and even the fellowship of the saints may be a guarantee of one's social respectability. It is because of this that the Divine *agape* is constantly needed to set right our human loves; the man who is in a right relation of *agape* with God must set right his personal relations with his neighbours, as our Lord taught both in the parable of the Unmerciful Servant and in the condition for forgiveness in the Lord's Prayer, and God alone can give him grace to do so. Forgiveness is here again at the heart of love.

There is a place in our human relationships for those aspects of love which have been given the label of *eros* as well as for those called *agape*. Our instinct to seek what is fair and lovely is a noble instinct, receiving apostolic commendation (Phil. iv.8). There may be a place even for *eros* in the form of a wise

[23] P. Philippe de la Sainte Trinité, quoted D'Arcy, *Mind and Heart of Love*, p. 321.
[24] P. Tillich, *Love, Power and Justice*, London 1954, p. 33.

self-love, although here there is much difference of opinion among thinkers. There is room in Christianity for the heavenly *eros* in its two characteristic Greek forms, that which seeks with Plato and the Hebrew Wisdom Literature to pursue the highest wisdom, and the more passionate *eros* that provided the nobler aspects of medieval romance and chivalry. (It may be admitted that of all forms of *eros* this is most liable to excess and perversion.) Yet all these forms of *eros* can flourish in a world without Christ; they were probably as vigorous in ancient Greece as they have ever been since. *Agape*, the love that gives itself for others, is in far greater danger of being crushed out in a fallen world. "You must look after yourself"; "Heaven helps those who help themselves"; "My religion is a private matter between me and my God"; "One should mind one's own business" are typical maxims by which worldly common sense tries to get rid of *agape*. Man's encounter with the forgiving love of God in Christ restores *agape* to its place at the head of the "loves," and it is only when it has this place that our human love becomes completely personal—the "I" responding to the "Thou" in perfect mutuality and full richness of emotional content. Thus all of real value that is wrongly sought for by self-love is attained. As Solovyov puts it: "Love as the actual abolition of egoism is the real justification and salvation of individuality."[25]

§ 4

There is a strange two-sidedness in the attitude of Christianity to the love of man and woman. On the one hand, it has been the esoteric symbol of the relation of the Church, or more dangerously of the individual soul, to Christ. St Paul expresses the fundamental truth here; "Husbands, love your wives, as Christ loved the Church, and gave himself up for her, that he might consecrate her, having cleansed her by the washing of water with the word" (Eph. v.25-6). Here we have the *agape* of God applied to human marriage in the giving up of oneself for the sake of the partner, in the selfless seeking of the partner's supreme good found in union with Christ, and in the forgiveness of wrongs symbolised in the cleansing of Baptism. In such a marriage the love between the sexes is both a training

[25] *A. Solovyov Anthology*, ed. S. L. Frank, London 1950, p. 157.

in *agape* and a provisional fulfilment of *agape* within human conditions and limitations. Solovyov sees in Christian marriage a realisation and incarnation of the Divine love; "In sexual love rightly understood and truly realised this divine essence finds a means for its complete and final embodiment in the individual life of man, for the deepest and at the same time most outwardly sensible and real union with him."[26] This, as St Paul said, is a great mystery, in the deepest sense of that word!

On the other hand, Christian thought has been reluctant to relate our human love between the sexes to the *agape* of God. For one thing *agape* is a universal love to all men, and a particular love, like that of husband and wife, may be regarded as likely to narrow the capacity for loving all men. In Catholic mystical piety, the love of God is sometimes set in complete contradiction to the love of the neighbour, so that the love of the creature must be abandoned when the love of God is reached. Even the Protestant Kierkegaard wrote; "Christianity has not come into the world to teach you how specifically to love your wife or your friend but ... how in common humanity you shall love all men. Love is a matter of conscience, and hence not a matter of impulse or inclination."[27] Behind all this there seems to be the view we have already referred to, that the *agape* of God has nothing to do with the love of Jesus for the beloved disciple. This is simply not true to Christian experience at its best; we may find the exceptional Mrs Jellyby who neglects her home in her devotion to the distant natives of Borrioboola Gha,[28] but there are far more Christian women whose enthusiasm for foreign missions is the outreaching of a love which has grown and developed in their care for their own homes and children. There is the danger, of course, that the love of the partner in marriage may take the place that belongs to the love of God alone, and then the marriage will certainly go sour. What is fundamentally wrong with this kind of argument is that the *agape* of God is not a universal benevolence, but a love that finds its greatest opportunities for self-giving, for its forgiving, and for its richest emotional warmth in the

[26] *Op. cit.*, p. 174.
[27] Quoted Niebuhr, *Christian Realism*, p. 150.
[28] C. Dickens, *Bleak House*.

personal encounters of human life—and most of all in the most intimate of human encounters, that of husband and wife.

Christians have often tended to regard sexual relations as carnal or unspiritual. Although this tradition has found a scriptural basis in the guarded counsels of St Paul to those living in the notoriously depraved atmosphere of Corinth (I Cor. vii.1), its real power lay in the Greek outlook with its emphasis on the dualism of soul and body, the body being definitely of a lower order than the soul. The Hebrew outlook, which seldom thought of soul and body as apart, and even then of the body as manifesting the activity of the soul, was entirely different.[29] We have seen the Greek outlook already in Plato's contrast between the vulgar, sexual *eros* and the heavenly *eros*. This Greek contempt of the flesh and consequently of the sexual instincts, although it is based on something older and more fundamental to our human nature than the Platonic philosophy, is certainly not evident in the Old Testament. This recognises sex as part of the order of Creation, accepts sex as a normal part of the life of its heroes, in which God takes an interest, without exaggerating that part, faces with an uncompromising realism and an outspoken condemnation the obvious dangers and perversions of sexual life, and sees and sympathises with its tragedies. This is the attitude to which our Lord was heir: He proclaimed as clearly as the author of Proverbs the dangers of the lustful glance, accepted the creative order as normative for monogamous marriage, and treated with compassion the victims of perverted sexuality. St Paul too, whatever he may have said to people in the vitiated circumstances of Corinth and however much his own position, as one called to be a eunuch for the Kingdom of Heaven's sake, may have biased his views on marriage, expresses in his letter to the Ephesians the happier and more truly biblical view.

A third factor in the depreciation of sexual relations was the exaltation of virginity. Here the early Christians were on firmer ground, for they had the example of our Lord Himself and His Virgin Mother before them. In the light of these examples none can doubt that there may be for some a vocation to the life of virginity, and that such a life, provided that it is filled with the love of God and of the brethren, may be even

---

[29] See A. R. Johnson, *The Vitality of the Individual in Ancient Israel*, Cardiff 1949.

richer and fuller than the lives of most married people. The acceptance of such a position implies no inferiority in those whose vocation is married life.

Christians see the obvious temptations, excesses, and perversions of sex, but to run away from these proves no solution of man's problem. Sex has often become an obsession in the minds of those who have shut it out of their lives, or has led to some strange perversions of religion. Some of man's sexual perversions are obscure and demonic, but many of them are simple and familiar sins. There is the use of the partner as a means, not merely to gross physical gratification, but, more subtly, to gain for oneself worldly security or position. There is the lack of any permanent satisfaction in a sexual life from which a spiritual partnership is excluded; bodily desire, like the horse-leech's daughters in Proverbs, cries; "Give, give" in an endless emptiness (Prov. xxx.15). There is the lack of readiness to forgive after God's example. There is the failure to set the love of God above even the most sacred of human ties, for without it the proportions of our human relationships go wrong. All this suggests that our sexual love must, like every other form of human love, be raised and transformed by the Divine *agape*. "There is certainly," writes Jean Guitton, "a continuity between the fire of human *Eros* and the flame of the Divine *Agape*. . . . But, that this unity may be realised, it is necessary that a higher love should descend to the lower love and become its guide. The lower love might, perhaps, be able to give the taste, the flavour and the first image of the celestial love; it is within the love of the senses like a luminous darkness; but this darkness cannot, of itself, give the light. Nature cannot lift herself up to that which surpasses her, unless that which surpasses comes down, in the form of grace and abides within her."[30] There is again an affinity between the love of man and woman and *agape* in that our human love is creative, not only in the way that animal love is creative, but also in that it is one of God's ways of soul-making. By the grace of God the experiences of married life can be a discipline and preparation for the life of heaven.

The normal outcome of married love is the family, and, here too, there is a two-sided attitude in Scripture. St Paul regards

[30] Guitton, *Essay on Human Love*, p. 196 f.

every human family as pointing back to "the Father from whom every family in heaven and on earth is named" (Eph. III.14-15), and, even in a fallen world, the relationships of the family show something of that *agape* between men, which should characterise the universal brotherhood of mankind. Yet Jesus definitely taught that the claims of one's human kin must always take second place to the love that we owe to God. In the end, "whoever does the will of God is my brother and sister and mother" (Mk. III.35; cf. Lk. XIV.26). The form that the corruption of the family has commonly taken is a narrow selfishness, seeking only the family's good. This has been aggravated in our own day by two factors. Small households have taken the place of the large households, either of the Eastern joint-family type or of the kind found formerly in this country which included a large household staff and often some relatives outside the immediate family circle. Such homes were more likely to be training grounds in a wider self-giving than the tiny households of today. Again the smaller number of children, now common, provides within itself less opportunity for the practice of *agape* between brothers and sisters. Ideally the love of the family should be the fountain of a more wide-spread *agape*. As Ruskin puts it; "For a noble woman, it [her home] stretches far round her, better than ceiled with cedar or painted with vermilion, shedding its quiet light far for those who else were homeless."[31]

§ 5

There is a Sibylline saying, "There is but one love," and the thesis of this chapter is that all genuine human love has its roots in the original order of Creation, the work of the Divine *agape*, and is capable of being restored and raised to the quality of Divine love by that same *agape* revealed in Christ. What this *agape* should mean for the Christian character and in practical Christian living has been stated so clearly by St Paul in I Cor. XIII and in Rom. XII as to need no comment. The restoration of such love can never be easy. For one thing love in its fulness implies mutuality, and even when one person gives himself in love to another, the other may reject his love. This was in the book of Hosea the tragedy both of God's love

[31] J. Ruskin, *Sesame and Lilies*, II, §68, 8th edn. Orpington 1887, p. 138.

to Israel and of Hosea's love to his wife, Gomer. Love, in the form of forgiveness which it must always take in a fallen world, is very costly; the Cross of Christ is the price of God's forgiving love. Love, too, means "the transformation of one's entire existence by God,"[32] and this means the love of God taking the first place in our lives. "Human love does not possess its own order and end within itself; it also should be suborainate to a higher love, which it symbolises and for which it should prepare the way."[33]

We end, where we began, with the love of God, but, except for the few whose vocation is the religious life, this love must be lived out in our common human relationships, in giving oneself for the other not only in the high adventure of martyrdom, but in the washing of the other's feet, and most of all, in the two spheres where love is most passionate and yet most precariously near to perversion, the love of man and woman, and the love of the family.

Literature

G. QUELL and E. STAUFFER, *Love*, Bible Key Words, London 1949.   Translation from G. Kittel, *Theologisches Wörterbuch zum Neuen Testament*.

A. NYGREN, *Agape and Eros*, London 1937, esp. VOL. I.   Translation of *Den kristna kärlekstanken*, Stockholm 1930.

J. MOFFATT, *Love in the New Testament*, London 1929.

C. S. LEWIS, *Christian Behaviour*, London 1943, ch. VIa.

W. LILLIE, *The Law of Christ*, London 1956, ch. X.

C. E. B. CRANFIELD, "Love," in *A Theological Word Book of the Bible*, ed. A. Richardson, London 1950.

C. SPICQ, *L'Agapè de I Cor. XIII*, Analecta Lovaniensia Biblica et Orientalia, ser. II, fasc. 48, Louvain 1954.

[32] Bonhoeffer, *Ethics*, p. 175.
[33] Guitton, *Essay on Human Love*, p. 231.

List of Abbreviated Titles used in Notes

BROMILEY, G. W., "Reconciliation"="The doctrine of reconciliation" in *Scottish Journal of Theology*, x (1957), pp. 76-85.

BUTLER, J., *Sermons*=J. Butler, *Fifteen Sermons preached at the Rolls Chapel*, in *Works*, ed. W. E. Gladstone, London 1896, VOL. II.

C. of S. *Report on Remarriage*, 1957=*Report of the Special Committee of the Church of Scotland on the Remarriage of Divorced Persons*, Edinburgh 1957.

CULLMANN, O., *State in N. T.*=*The State in the New Testament*, London 1957.

DAUBE, D., *N.T. and Rabbinic Judaism*=*The New Testament and Rabbinic Judaism*, London 1956.

ELLUL, J., *Presence*=*The Presence of the Kingdom*, London 1951. Translation of *Présence au monde moderne*, Geneva 1948.

ELLUL, J., *Theological Foundation*=*The Theological Foundation of Law*, London 1961. Translation of *Le Fondement théologique du droit*, Neuchâtel 1946.

LEBRETON, J., "Renoncement dans le N.T."="La doctrine du renoncement dans le Nouveau Testament," in *Nouvelle revue théologique*, LXV (1938), pp. 385-412.

MARSHALL, L. H., *N.T. Ethics*=*The Challenge of New Testament Ethics*, London 1948.

NIEBUHR, R., *Christian Realism*=*Christian Realism and Political Problems*, London 1954.

PIERCE, C. A., *Conscience in N.T.*=*Conscience in the New Testament*. Studies in Biblical Theology VOL. XV, London 1955.

RICHARDSON, A., *Work*=*The Biblical Doctrine of Work*. Ecumenical Biblical Studies VOL. I, London 1952.

WILDER, A. N., *Eschatology and Ethics*=*Eschatology and Ethics in the teaching of Jesus*, revised edition, New York 1950.

Index of Scripture References

Gen. I.3	19	Ru. IV.16	6 n.
I.27	121		
I.28	108, 117	I Sam. V	2
II.24	120, 121, 126, 127	VIII.10-17	85
III.21	166	XII.12	82
XII.3	7	XVIII.3	9
XVIII.1-15	166	XVIII.8	9
XVIII.25	70 n.	XX.13-16	9
XX.5 f.	46	XXIV.5	46
XXIX.31	166 n.	XXV.25	58
XXXI.44	9		
XXXI.50	9	II Sam. VI.6-9	2
XXXI.53	9		
		I Kgs. III.6	46 n.
Ex. XXIV.1-8	9	IX.4	46
XXIV.6	9		
XXIV.8	9	II Kgs. XXIII.3	9
XXXV.31	105		
		II Chron. XX.7	167
Lev. XIX.2	2, 3		
XIX.18	1	Neh. IX.38	9
XXI.7	119		
XXI.14	119	Job	93
		XXVII.6	46
Deut. IV.39	58	XLII.5 f.	2
VI.5	1		
IX.5	46 n.	Ps. I.3	93
XV.15	3	CIV.23	108
XXII	118	CXIX	79
XXII.8	75	CXIX.7	46 n.
XXIII.19 f.	94	CXIX.127 f.	58
XXIV.1-4	121	CXLIII	5 n.
XXIV.4	120		
		Prov. III.34	131
Jos. VIII.	10	IV.10	169
XXIV.25	9	XXX.15	179
Jud. V.11	4		

N

Eccles.	175	Mat. I.19	119
		III.2	142
		IV.17	142
Is. III.14-16	93	V.3-12	143
v.8-12	93	V.3	95
VI.5	2	V.16	37
XLII.1	167	V.17-20	72
XLIII.10	58	V.18	1, 72
XLIX.24	4	V.31 f.	123, 124
LX.4	6 n.	V.39	17 n.
		V.40	78
		V.45	19, 39
Jer. I.5	58	V.48	3, 25
XXXI.31	9	VI.1-18	59, 148
XXXI.33	18	VI.1	62
XXXI.34	146	VI.2	62, 78
		VI.5	62
		VI.12	175
Ezk. II.1	40	VI.14 f.	6
XXXIII	145 n.	VI.19-21	97
XLVI	88	VI.19	102
		VI.24	97, 109
		VI.32	93, 97
Hos.	180 f.	VI.33	102, 113
II.19 f.	166	VII.1	43
VI.6	58	VII.24-7	34
XI.3 f.	166	X.35	137
		X.38	99, 151
		X.39	161
		X.40	130
Amos III.2	58	X.42	130
IV.1	93	XI.16 f.	130
V.11 f.	93	XI.19	156
VI.4-6	93	XI.25	17, 57, 67
VIII.4-6	93	XI. 26	57
		XI.29	24, 30, 131, 158 n.
		XII.43-55	159
Hab. II.4	6	XVI.3	61
		XVI.24	99, 151
		XVI.27	147
Mal. I.2 f.	166	XVIII.3	131
		XVIII.4	130 f.
		XVIII.22	22
W. of Sol.VI.3	87	XVIII.23-35	175
XVII.11	46	XIX.2-8	120
		XIX.3-12	124
		XIX.6	124
Ecc. XXVIII.34	112	XIX.9	123

Mat. XIX.10-12	125	Mk. X.25	156
XX.1-16	109	X.41 f.	29
XXII.15-22	59	XII.13-17	59, 91
XXIII.	60	XIII.10	142
XXIII.1-4	59	XIII.30	148
XXIII.15	60	XIV.3-9	28, 32, 156
XXIII.16 f.	60	XIV.36	115
XXIII.23	59		
XXIII.26	60		
XXIII.27	59	Lk. I.38	172
XXV.14-30	105	II.39-51	28
XXV.31-46	147	II.41-8	137
XXVI.52	17 n	II.51	32, 133
XXVI.53	83	II.52	132
		III.12-14	110
		IV.16	32
		V.8	2, 154
Mk. I.20	109	VI.15	83
I.21-34	32	VI.20	95
I.35	32	VI.32-5	94
II.23-8	71, 72	VI.36	3, 25
II.27 f.	113	VI.38	93
III.16	33	IX.23	99, 151
III.17	33, 154	IX.49-56	29
III.21	137	IX.59 f.	138
III.31-4	137	X.7	110
III.35	180	X.21	67
V.43	28	X.29-37	29, 74, 79, 167 f., 174
VI.3	27, 28, 110, 137	XII.15	96, 98
VII.1-23	72	XII.16-21	97
VII.9	59	XII.33 f.	93
VII.11-13.	135	XII.56	61
VII.13	61, 71	XIII.32	90
VIII.22	58	XIV.26	137, 166, 180
VIII.33	154	XIV.27	99, 151, 158
VIII.34	24, 30, 99, 151, 158	XV.11-32	21, 70, 163
VIII.35	153	XV.17	109
IX.1	148	XVI.1-15	100 f.
IX.37	130	XVI.9	97
IX.42	129, 130	XVI.18	123
X.2-12	17, 72, 120	XVI.19-31	97, 143
X.5	16	XIX.1-10	54, 154
X.6	15, 22	XIX.8 f.	91
X.11 f.	122, 125	XX.20-6	59
X.12	119, 123 f.	XXII.25	92
X.14	129	XXIII.2	83
X.17-22	99	XXIII.34	88
X.23-6	95 f.		

Jn. III.3	132	Rom. II.14-6	13 f.
III.17	69	II.14	73
IV.17 f.	154	II.15	51, 54, 71
V.22	69	II.20	73
V.27	69	III.20	77
V.30	69	III.20 f.	73
VI.27-9	106	III.23	43
VI.27	112	IV.15	73, 76
VII.48 f.	58	V.5	163
VIII.1-11	16, 71	V.8	169
IX.4	108	V.20	73, 76
XI.5	166	VI	159
XII.20	164	VI.4	160
XII.24 f.	20	VI.8	158
XII.25	99, 151	VI.14	73
XIII.1-3	30	VI.16	77
XIII.1-15	28	VII	64
XIII.15	25	VII.5 f.	76
XIII.23	166	VII.7	74
XIII.34	25	VII.12	75
XIII.35	8	VII.14	75
XVI.8-11	54 f.	VII.19	34
XVI.13	54	VII.23	73
XVI.14	170	VII.24	36
XVII.3	64	VIII.2	73
XVII.26	160, 172	VIII.3 f.	72
XVIII.33-8	84	IX.1	55
XVIII.36	17 n.	IX.30 f.	22 n.
XIX.25-7	137	X, XI	84
		X.4	73
		XII	180
Acts II.44 f.	17	XII.6-8	107
IV.32-7	103	XIII.1-7	80, 86, 88, 90, 91
V.3-5	103	XIII.1	15, 71, 73
V.36 f.	83	XIII.4	73
XVII.30	57	XIII.5	48, 50
XVIII.3	110	XIII.6	87, 112
XXI.38	83	XIII.7 f.	92
XXIII.1	53	XIV.5	51
XXIV.16	53, 54	XIV.17	98
		XV.9	37
Rom. I.1	37		
I.7	169	1 Cor. I.2	37, 146
I.18-32	13, 15 f.	II.8	88
I.18	17	III.1-3	132
I.26 f.	15	III.9	106
II.12	73	IV.4	53

1 Cor. v.2	160	Gal. III.24 f.	73
v.9 f.	112	IV.1 f.	109
VI.1-6	88	IV.21-V.1	77
VI.16	127	IV.21	72
VII	125, 144	V.1	79
VII.1	178	V.13	111
VII.10	124	V.18	73
VII.10 f.	125	VI.2	78
VII.14	129	VI.16	84
VII.20	106 n.		
VII.39	126		
VIII	50 ff.		
VIII.1	63	Eph. I.17 f.	64
IX.7	13	III.14 f.	180
IX.19-23.	78	III.15	15
IX.27	35, 102, 153	IV.11	107
X.14-30	49, 51	IV.14	133
XI.1	24	IV.18	57
XI.14-16	18	IV.28	110, 111
XI.25	9	V.1	26, 35
XI.31	43	V.12	16 n.
XII.26	160	V.21-VI.9	109
XII.28	107	V.21-33	126
XIII	180, 181	V.22 f.	128
XIV.20	133	V.25 f.	176
XV.34	57	V.29	151
XV.58	114, 142	V.32	126
XVI.2	101	VI.1-4	129
		VI.1	133
		VI.3	135
II Cor. I.12	47	VI.4	133, 136
IV.2	47	VI.5-8	101, 109
V.1	106	VI.5	114
V.10	69, 147	VI.12	144
V.11	47		
V.14	163		
V.17	160		
VIII.9	29, 101	Phil. II.4	37
IX.12	113	II.5-8	29
X.1	131	II.7	110
XII.14	135	II.12	35
		II.12 f.	106, 141 f.
		II.17	113
		II.30	113
Gal. II.16	77	III.12	35
II.19	73	III.20	85, 146
II.20	37, 158, 159, 160, 164	IV.8	105, 175
III.11	77		

Col. II.8-23	63	Tit. I.15		51
II.18	41	II.3-8		128
III.2	92, 98	II.9		114
III.3-5	160	II.10		110
III.5	97	III.1 f.		86
III.18-IV.1	109			
III.18 f.	128			
III.20 f.	129, 133	Heb. II.10		170
III.22-5	101	IV		113
III.22	114	V.8		133
III.23 f.	109	XII.6	70, 136,	169
IV.11	141	XIII.18		53
I. Thess.I.3	106			
IV.15	148	Jas. II.6		93
V.19	51	IV.6		131
V.22	35	V.2 f.		97
		V.4		94
II Thess. II.7	87			
III.6-13	144	I Pet. I.14		58
III.8-12	108	II.12		12
		II.13-17		86
I Tim. I.5	53	II.13-25		89
I.19	53	II.16		89
II.1 f.	86, 89	II.18-III.7		109
III.3	98	II.19	47,	50
III.9	53	II.20		114
IV.2	51	II.21-3		24
V.4	135	II.23	30,	114
V.18	110	III.1-7		128
VI.1	110, 114	III.16		53
VI.9 f.	98	III.21		53
VI.17	97	V.2		98
		V.5		131
II Tim. I.3	53			
I.5	137	I Jn. III.2 f.		25
III.14-17	137	III.17		31
		IV.9-11		30
		IV.11		163
Tit. I.7	98	IV.16		163
I.11	98	IV.18		169
I.14	52	V.3		172

II Jn. 7	63	Rev. XVI.13	89
		XVII.1	90
		XVII.5	90
Rev. II.6	65	XVIII.17	97
II.15	65	XIX.20	89
XIII	89	XX.10	89
XIV.13	114, 142	XXI.2	116, 141

PRINTED IN GREAT BRITAIN BY
OLIVER AND BOYD LTD.
EDINBURGH